TRANSFERABLE TABLE

always to be placed opposite the page which is being studied in the book of exercises, thus enabling the variants heading each example to be put into practice

1. Table of the twelve major and twelve minor scales for use in daily transposition, classed in chromatic sequences.

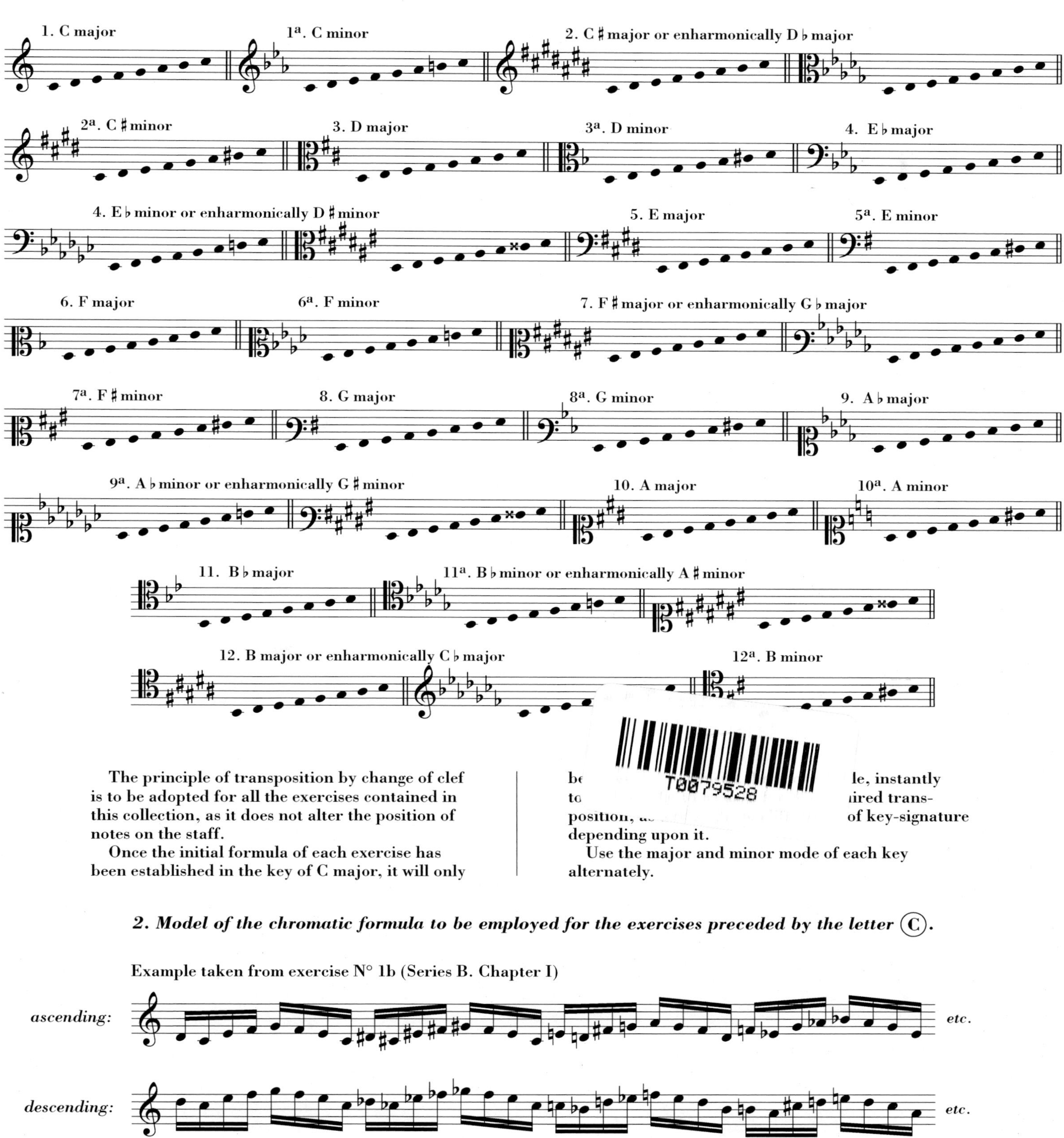

The principle of transposition by change of clef is to be adopted for all the exercises contained in this collection, as it does not alter the position of notes on the staff.

Once the initial formula of each exercise has been established in the key of C major, it will only be [illegible] le, instantly to [illegible] ired transposition, a[illegible] of key-signature depending upon it.

Use the major and minor mode of each key alternately.

2. Model of the chromatic formula to be employed for the exercises preceded by the letter Ⓒ.

Example taken from exercise N° 1b (Series B. Chapter I)

3. Table of harmonic combinations for the successive study of all the formulae preceded by the letter Ⓗ.

Examples taken from exercise N° 1b (Series B. Chapter I) demonstrating the use of the Table of harmonic combination on 5 notes, with the original fingering retained

(same process for the exercises established on successions of 3 or 4 notes.)

4. Table of the different rhythms to be used in the study of the exercises preceded by the letter Ⓡ.

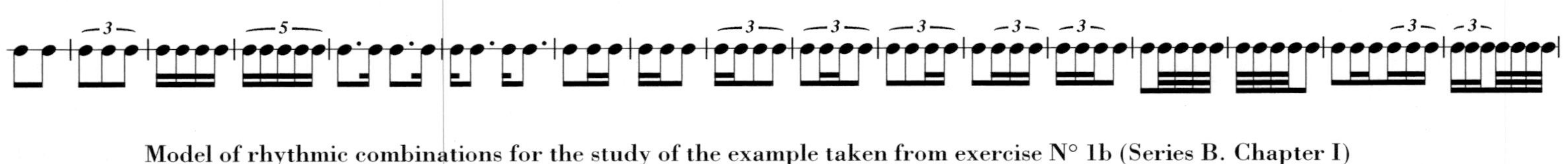

Model of rhythmic combinations for the study of the example taken from exercise N° 1b (Series B. Chapter I)

5. Table of the fingerings to be used in the exercises preceded by the letter Ⓕ.

2 fingers: 1 2, 1 3, 1 4, 1 5 — 2 3, 2 4, 2 5, — 3 4, 3 5 — 4 5

3 fingers: 1 2 3, 1 2 4, 1 2 5 — 1 3 4, 1 3 5 — 1 4 5 — 2 3 4, 2 3 5, 2 4 5 — 3 4 5

4 fingers: 1 2 3 4 — 1 2 3 5 — 1 3 4 5 — 2 3 4 5

5 fingers: 1 2 3 4 5 — 1 2 4 3 5 — 1 2 5 4 3 — 1 2 5 3 4 — 1 2 3 5 4 — 1 2 4 5 3
1 3 2 4 5 — 1 3 4 2 5 — 1 3 5 2 4 — 1 3 5 4 2 — 1 3 2 5 4 — 1 3 5 4 2
1 4 3 2 5 — 1 4 2 3 5 — 1 4 5 2 3 — 1 4 5 3 2 — 1 4 3 5 2 — 1 4 2 5 3
1 5 4 3 2 — 1 5 3 2 4 — 1 5 3 4 2 — 1 5 2 3 4 — 1 5 4 2 3 — 1 5 2 4 3

(same fingerings, in reverse order for the left hand)

These combinations can be renewed by beginning each group with a different finger and transferring the fingers momentarily omitted, to the end of the formula.

Example (Exercise N° 5 Series B. Chapter II)

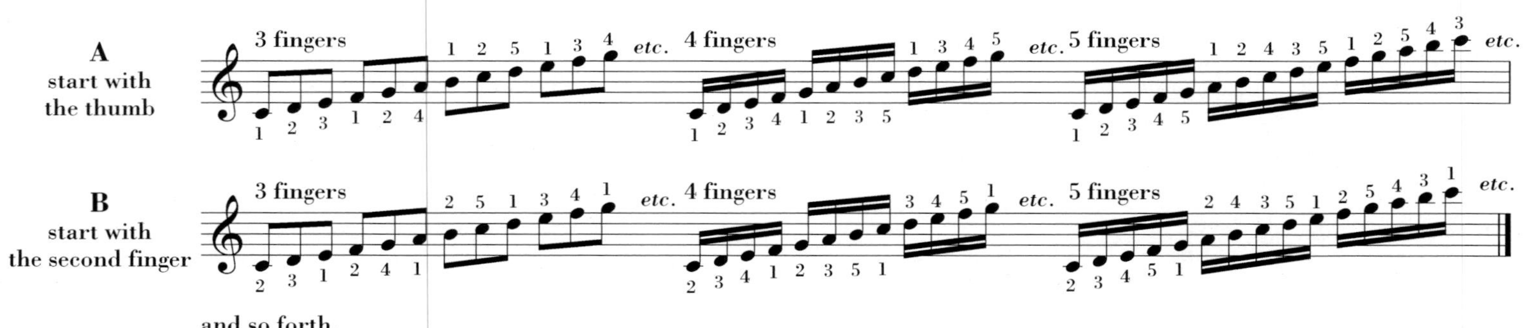

and so forth.

Alfred

CORTOT

Rational principles of pianoforte technique

translated by R. LE ROY - METAXAS

ÉDITIONS SALABERT

INDEX

ALFRED CORTOT

Rational Principles of Pianoforte Technique

FOREWORD

Two factors form the basis of any instrumental study — one psychological factor from which arise taste, imagination, reasoning, the feeling for shading and tone : in a word, style — one physiological factor, that is, dexterity of the hands and fingers, absolute submission of the muscles and nerves to the material exigencies of execution.

For the development of the psychological side, which is above all a function of personality and taste, pedagogy can rely only upon the enrichment of general culture, upon the development of the imaginative and analytical faculties which open the way to the translation of the emotions and sensations evoked by music.

For this purpose there exist neither good nor bad systems, but only good and bad teachers.

On the other hand, endless collections of exercises of every kind solicit the zeal of pianists anxious to acquire mechanical mastery of the keyboard.

There is, speaking literally, an overwhelming choice of these works. We should certainly never have considered adding a new element of perplexity to this imposing collection of contradictory theories, through which the problem of pianistic technique is seen wearing the terrific aspect of a hundred-headed hydra, had not our especial care been that of simplifying the question and demonstrating the vulnerability of the monster.

One of the most significant points in the progress of instrumental teaching during the last few years, is that the mechanical and long-repeated practice of a difficult passage has been replaced by the reasoned study of the difficulty contained therein, reduced to its elementary principle.

With this fact in view, we have established a method of work whose laws we have attempted to apply in our edition of the works of Chopin.

We shall try, in the following pages, to generalise a formula, whose efficiency several years of experience have allowed us to test, by extending it to pianistic difficulties of every order, reducing the latter to five categories, each of which will be analysed in a separate chapter. That is to say, that instead of pursuing virtuosity along the uncertain paths of complication and ever-increasing technical difficulty, we shall seek on the contrary, making use of the valuable examples afforded us by athletic training, to retain only those movements which are indispensable to its complete development.

It will thus become possible to review every morning, in the space of about an hour, the complete cycle of the problems of piano-playing. No doubt these daily gymnastics for the pianist will be compared to the series of physical and respiratory exercises prescribed by hygienists. Such a comparison, even made ironically, cannot fail to please us. It perfectly defines the object and utility of this work.

PLAN FOR THE STUDY OF THE EXERCISES.

1. A preparatory period of six months is necessary for a thorough preliminary study of this collection, consisting of three quarters of an hour's work each day, and of about a month, or, more accurately, thirty-six consecutive days for the preparation of each chapter; a quarter of an hour's work should be devoted regularly, apart from any other category of exercise, every day, to the preparatory chapter entitled « Daily Keyboard Gymnastics », whose object is the reasoned loosening of all the pianist's muscular apparatus, that is to say, fingers, hand, wrist and even forearm; a total of one hour is thus obtained, to be reserved for technical problems in the work of each day.

During this first period of study, the anticipation of any chapter by a succeeding one must be absolutely avoided, all modification in the established plan being in radical opposition to the essential object of this work, which is the complete assimilation of the principle of each difficulty taken separately.

2. There is nothing arbitrary in the division of the work of each chapter into periods of thirty-six days. This is determined by adopting a different key as the starting-point for the work of each day, and since the chromatic scale is composed of twelve sounds, there will be three divisions of twelve days each.

During the first twelve days, Series A of the chapter under attention should be studied (first day : C major and C minor, second day : C sharp major and C sharp minor, and so forth); during the twelve following days Series B in the same fashion — then for the last twelve days, Series C.

Daily chromatic transposition has the effect of constantly renewing the position of the fingers on the keyboard, and the fingering of the key of C, according to which all the formulae have been initially established, should be preserved in every key.

This principle of daily transposition is strictly compulsory.

3. From the sixth month onward the study of the various difficulties should be mixed, either by the daily selection from each chapter, of the Series bearing the same letter, or else by taking them in contrary order. to avoid accustoming the fingers to the repetition of formulae invariably presented in the same sequence.

The familiarity by now acquired, with the different categories of exercises, will permit of their unhesitating succession, and this circuit of the pianoforte's difficulties can be effected in about an hour, including the daily repetition of the chapter dealing with the gymnastics of the keyboard, never on any account to be neglected.

The principle of daily transposition will, of course, be preserved in the new distribution of the exercises. That is to say, that by embarking every day on a new key, twelve days will again be necessary to exhaust the modulatory cycle of each combination. But this mode of procedure can equally be alternated with the repetition on every degree of the chromatic scale, that is twelve times for each formula, of certain exercises designated by conventional signs whose meaning is given below.

In the same way, fingering, rythm, and harmonic basis of each exercise can be renewed « ad infinitum », according to the indications on the transferable table of reference to which these signs refer.

It is impossible to lay sufficient stress on the importance of a complete rest of ten minutes duration, after the study of these exercises and before undertaking any new work.

Physical effort, if not followed by complete muscular relaxation, is prejudicial to any form of training.

It is thus that the technical formula, whose regular use will ensure the upkeep of a thoroughly supple mechanism, docile to every exigency of execution, will henceforward be presented.

4. But at this point there intervenes, under the teacher's control, the individual participation of the pupil.

Even though we fully take into account the purely physiological character of the work whose foundations we lay down in this volume, we cannot possibly admit of any neglect in reflection or discernment.

We therefore leave blank at the end of each chapter two pages of ruled paper reserved for the noting of new formulae of exercises having relation to the difficulty dealt with in the chapter and due either to the ingenuity of the pupil or to the initiative of the master.

The latter will indeed have been able, during the first period of six months dedicated to the preparatory study of this collection, to discern precisely which are the weak places in the technique submitted to his control. It will thus be possible for him eventually to insist with, as it were, scientific authority, upon certain details of mechanism to which special work should be devoted..

We consider that it would not be out of place to remind the reader at this point, of that principle of pianoforte instruction, too rarely applied in our opinion, namely that, according to the formation of the hands, their adaptation to the keyboard may be — indeed, must be — distinctly different.

A summary classification of the different types of hand sufficiently explicit, however, to avoid being equivocal — hands with long fingers or hands with short fingers — will serve as a point of departure for the particular direction of the pupils' studies. Adopting a method of work, specialised in this way, should permit of a fairly rapid amendment of certain faults, which, at first sight might seem impossible to overcome, even by means of the most stubborn work.

In fact, we may confidently affirm that no physical obstacle exists in pianistic execution, which is absolutely insurmountable, when once the nature of the obstacle has been clearly defined, and when reason and logic have been called upon for its conquest.

In order to open the way to useful research in the direction we have just pointed out, we mention at the end of each chapter the exercises which apply especially to the various formations of the hand described above.

We also append, at the end of this work, by way of an indication, a summary repertory of works preferably chosen from classical pianoforte literature, the study of which will permit of the immediate application of the technical principle analysed in each chapter. The teacher must decide for himself, in what measure and at what moment, it will be fitting to have recourse to this complementary study.

We take the liberty of advising him to follow the example, in this matter, of a perspicacious doctor who, according to the constitution of his patient, refrains from using the same therapeutic measures for one whose appearance is analagous.

5. One final observation with regard to the transferable table of reference which should act as a guide for the systematic study of each chapter, and which should be placed opposite each page under attention.

Upon it we have placed :

1. A table of the twelve major and minor scales to be used in turn for daily transposition, the point of departure for each exercise being raised by one chromatic degree every day.

As this system is common to all the examples in the collection we have dispensed with a special sign such as those which will be found below.

2. A model of the chromatic formula to be employed for the exercises preceded by the letter (C) (daily transposition on to all the degrees of the chromatic scale).

3. A table of the harmonic combinations according to which all the formulae preceded by the letter (H) are to be studied as well as a model of the modifications to which the use of a new disposal may give rise.

4. A table of the different rhythms to be applied to the formulae preceded by the letter (R) and a model of combined rhythms.

5. A table of the different fingerings which it will be necessary to use in succession for the study of the formulae preceded by the letter (F) and a model for the application of various fingerings to the same formula.

When the same exercise is accompanied by one or more of these letters or conventional signs, this means that the exercise may studied indiscriminately according to the tables referred to by these letters, and that these tables may either be used in succession or in conjunction.

Finally we recall the fact that except where otherwise specified, all the exercises are applicable to both hands, the fingerings for the right hand being given above the notes, and for the left hand below them.

The examples for the left hand are usually written in the treble clef in order to allow the use of the transposition table.

Nevertheless, and the same applies to all the exercises in this collection, either for both hands or for one, we recommend that they should be studied with frequent changes of octave, which has the effect of accustoming the hand to all the positions which it can possibly take up on they keyboard.

Most of the exercises in this work are reversible. That is to say that it will suffice to use the fingering for the right hand in the left or vice versa, and to follow the order of the fingers according to the harmonic formula that is chosen, to give birth to a new disposal.

In the course of study it will be noticed that the modifications we have just indicated will enable the formulae, which are to a certain extent impersonal, to be constantly varied, and their interest and utility diversified.

We have not so much attempted in writing the following exercises to invent new ones, as to obtain from the simplest of them, by a systematic method, the maximum of pianistic efficiency.

It is the way in which they are studied, and not the actual substance of them, which confers a special value upon them, and, to make use of an ambitious metaphor, enlarges their horizon.

Daily Keyboard Gymnastics

Preliminary Chapter Dedicated to the Study of Movements of the Fingers, Hand, and Wrist.

The sole object of the exercises contained in this chapter is to render the fingers, hand and wrist supple, with a view to their adaptation to the keys apart from any application of a musical order.

They constitute real instrumental gymnastics; and no words are sufficient to insist on the necessity of consecrating a quarter of an hour to them daily before any other study.

The metronome numbers indicated, as well as the repetitions of each exercise are worked out with this duration in view.

EXERCISE No 1. (*Independence of the fingers. Control of their individual movements*).

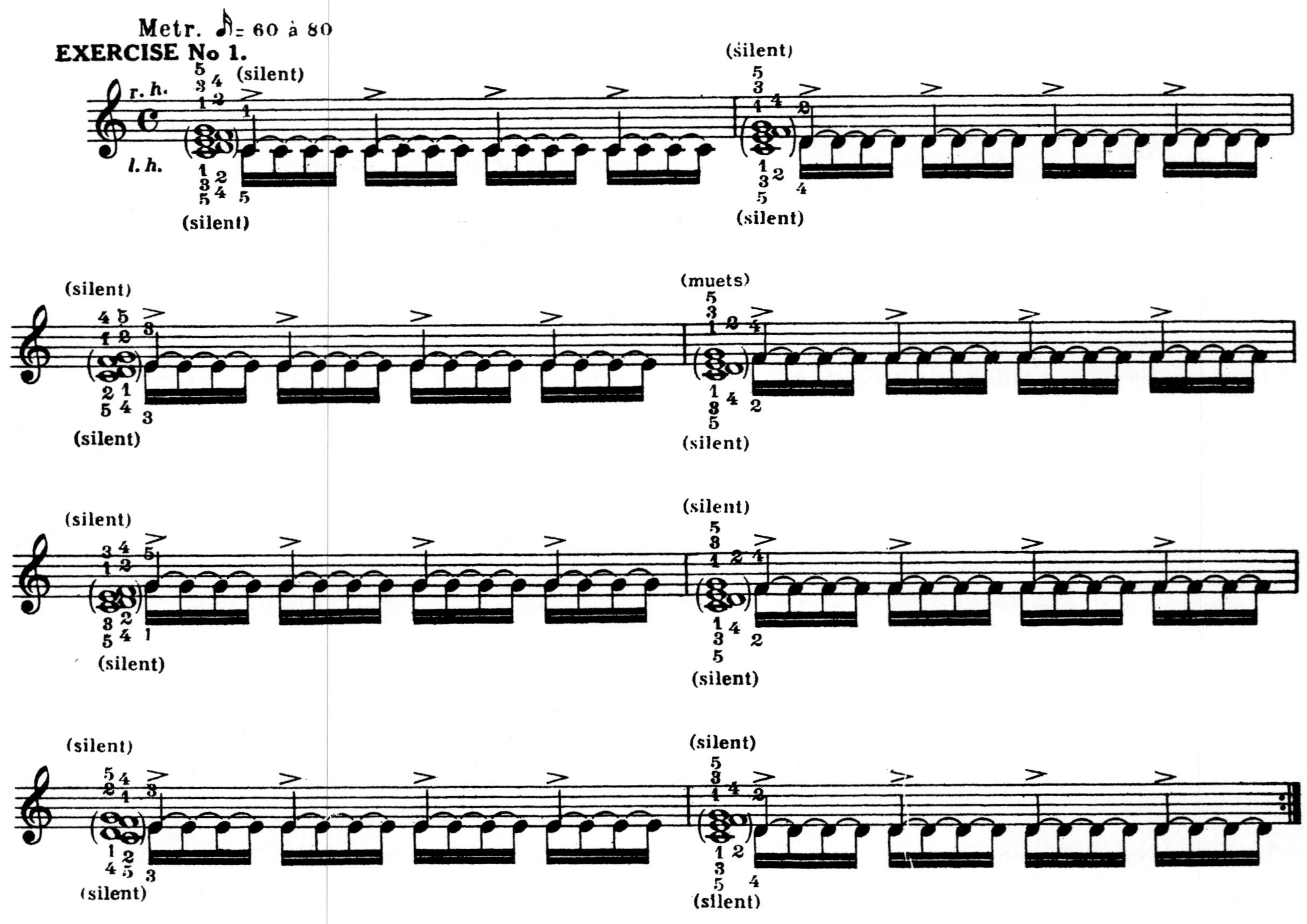

Place the fingers on the keys marked with semi-breves, without pressing them down. Then, leaving the other fingers in silent contact with the keys, resting lightly on their surface, lower each finger affected by the execution of the semi-quavers, counting four on each crotchet :

1, to strike the note, — 2, to press the finger down as far as the key will go (without cramping or stiffening the other fingers) — 3, to let the key rise with the finger, — 4, to cease the pressure. This exercise is to be studied in the four following positions, a different position being adopted daily.

to be transposed into every key.

(The same system of work for exercises No. 2 & 3, 1a, 2a, 3a.)

EXERCISE No 2 (*Development of the muscles of the fingers*).

This exercise is played on the same notes as the preceding one, keeping the silent position of the fingers on the semi-breves. But the finger which executes the semi-quavers will describe the following movements, still counting 4 on each crotchet, and in the given metronomic movement : 1, to strike the note — 2, to slide the finger in action below the level of the motionless fingers, relinquishing the key and stretching it downwards as far as possible, perpendicularly, in front of the key-board — 3, to bring the finger back to the level of the keys — 4, to lift the finger vertically, as high as possible.

In this exercise the active finger only remains in contact with the key for the duration of the first semi-quaver of each beat.

EXERCISE No 3 (*Lateral finger movements to give suppleness to the flexor of the fingers*).

Exercises based on the same formula with the same metronomic movement and the same number of repetitions for each position.

The active finger, in this case, executes the following movements : 1, to sound the note — 2, to stretch the extended finger to the left, crossing it over the other fingers and as far as possible — 3, the same movement to the right — 4, to raise it vertically above its key. Only the thumb's movements differ from those just described, owing to its especial conformation. It should be brought to the right for the right hand, to the left for the left hand, passing under the fingers instead of over them. These three exercises must be exclusively practised *piano*.

The same formula as for Exercises 1, 2, and 3, but with fingers pressed down, lowering the keys as far as they will go.

Practise these : *m.f.* and *f*.

EXERCISE No 4 (*To give suppleness to the lateral movements of the wrist.*)

Strike each chord neatly, taking care to attack all the notes simultaneously, then subject the wrist (which must remain absolutely loose) to a combined flexuous and rotary movement, up-and-down and from left to right, for the right hand, and from right to left for the left hand, executing one complete movement for each crotchet, that is : four movements in each bar.

Maintain the position of each finger firmly upon the keys and let the wrist describe as pronounced a circular movement as possible. Afterwards reverse the movement of the wrist, that is to say work it from right to left for the right hand and from left to right for the left hand.

EXERCISE No 5 (*Giving suppleness to the horizontal movements of the wrist; flexibility of the hand*).

On the same succession of chords.

After striking each chord raise the wrist and push it towards the back of the key-board, so as to overturn the fingers forwards, with the wrist higher up than the back of the hand, then draw back the wrist towards the body, until the fingers are flat upon the keys. Repeat this backward forward and movement, which must be executed with suppleness and decision, the extremities of the fingers never leaving their original position upon the keys. describing a complete movement for every quaver.

Tempo : Metr=60. Keep the keys pressed down all the time.

EXERCISE No 6.

The same exercise reversed; that is to say : slide the hand towards the back of the key-board, lifting the finger-tips as high as possible so that their inner surface presses upright against the panel behind the key-board, then bring back the hand. and let the fingers regain their curved position. The wrist must be lowered as the hand advances and must be raised as it returns to its original position.

It will be advantageous in this exercise to keep one finger in contact with its key in its normal position, and to use each finger in succession in this way.

EXERCISE No 7 (*To develop a firm attack of the fingers, while keeping a supple wrist*).

Use the chords in the formula given for Exercise No. 4. Press down all the fingers, taking care that all the notes are struck simultaneously, then, with the exception of one finger which remains in contact with its key, lower the hand as far as possible below the level of the key-board, keeping the free fingers folded back towards the palm of the hand.

Use each of the five fingers in succession to hold the single note on each chord formation, and repeat the movement four times after each change of finger.

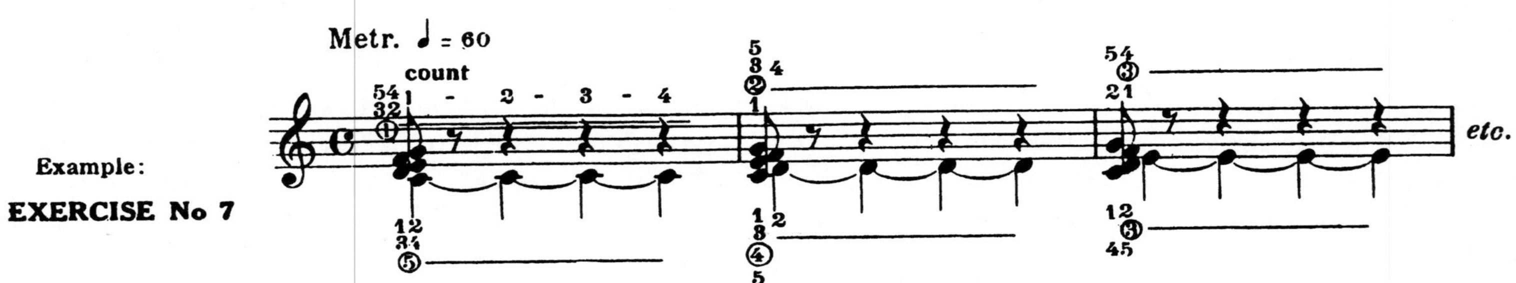

EXERCISE No 8 (*Suppleness of the wrist and forearm : vertical movement*).

Hold the hands at the level of the shoulders, then, with a rapid and decided movement throw them on to the key-board which they must brush lightly without sounding any notes, immediately rebounding to their original position where they should make a slight pause. Repeat this gesture twenty times at the rate of 60 for each movement.

EXERCISE No 9 (*Suppleness and rapidity of lateral movements of the forearm: flexibility of the elbow*).

The object of this exercise is to develop the lateral mobility of the forearm, with a view to adapting it to a rapid technique in the transmission of the hand along the key-board. This is to be accomplished as follows : place the right hand on the key-board, as far to the left as possible and throw it, by means of a supple movement of the forearm, towards the highest keys on the extreme right; then return it to its starting point. Make a slight pause on arriving at each extremity. Afterwards execute the same movement in the opposite direction with the left hand. The time is the same as that of the preceding exercise. Repeat each movement 20 times.

Except for Exercise No. 9 these exercises are to be practised with both hands together. The principle of daily transposition is to be applied, and also frequent changes of octave.

As the foregoing exercises are based upon a purely physiological conception of manual gymnastics applied to the piano, we feel it indispensable to exact the perfect posture of the body for their execution, of which this is the compulsory corollary, and the only means of giving absolute accuracy and amplitude to the movements which we have indicated.

With this object in view we draw the attention of teachers to the necessity of insisting that the pupil should use a seat whose height is exactly suited to his physical constitution.

The key-board being generally 28 1/2 in. from the floor (we are speaking of grand pianofortes only, for the most unexpected differences exist in the height of the key-boards of upright pianofortes), the normal height of the seat for a pupil of average stature can be estimated at 18 ins. The lenght of the arm even more than that of the body should determine the correct conditions of accomodation at the key-board. The arm should be bent in a natural curve in such a way as to avoid those troublesome angles which paralyse the normal play of the muscles of the forearm and of the hand.

As a general rule the wrist should be held less high than the hand: the naturally curved position of he index-finger on the key will fix that of the other fingers, which, as far as their unequal length will permit, without injurious contraction, should strike the respective keys on the same level and at the same point. Exaggerated articulation and disastrous stiffiness will thus be avoided.

Contact with the keys will naturally be established by the largest possible surface of the small phalanx.

In the work known as "Articulation , certain teachers demand a greater output of strength, from their puipls, in raising the finger above the key-board, than in pressing the key down. May we be allowed to give the lie to the efficiency of this utterly anti-physiological system.

Rational Principles of Pianoforte Technique.

In the beginning of this work, we stated that we thought it possiblè to group all the problems of pianistic execution into five essential categories. We conceive this classification in the following manner :

1. Equality, independence and mobility of fingers.
2. Passing under of the thumb (scales-arpeggios).
3. Double notes and polyphonic playing.
4. Extensions.
5. Wrist technique, execution of chords.

We consider that in the whole literature of the pianoforte, no difficulty exists which cannot be placed under one of the preceding headings.

We are also convinced that an attentive study of the following pages will determine an appropriate method of work for every difficulty.

The interpretation of music by means of a docile and supple mechanism, the conscientious servant of the thought to be conveyed, will thus become possible.

But this, we repeat with emphasis, can be attained on one condition only : that of conforming exactly to the plan of work which we prescribe; without abusing the economy of its system by unseemly haste; without imagining that the alternative anticipation of a preceding chapter by another would give quicker and more conclusive results; without prematurely abandoning any exercise with the idea that its particular difficulty has been easily overcome; and lastly, without exaggerating through laudable but misplaced excess of zeal, the duration of the daily task set by us.

As to the reward to be expected from the patient effort we demand, we would willingly define it by quoting the words of Garcia to the youthful Malibran, liberating her from the lengthy and severe vocal exercises to which he had subjected her : "And now go—and sing according to your heart—you know your trade".

CHAPTER I

Equality, Independence and Mobility of the Fingers (Without Passing under of the Thumb)

The object of the exercises contained in this chapter is the development of the virtuosity on which key-board technique was founded up to the advent of Beethovenian romanticism : that is to say the light and airy virtuosity of the Harpsichord players, all trembling with a winged life of trills, mordants, roulades, and grupetti, such as that of Couperin, Scarlatti and Rameau.

The style of a Bach, a Haydn, a Mozart, although more meditative, more ardently eloquent, is nevertheless also a tributary of the sonorous rhetoric resulting from the particular resources of the instruments of the period.

It is the epoch of even and running execution: when the virtuoso's ambition was to imitate the amiable manner of the singer, the elegant vivacity of his art, with its wealth of embellishments and flowery grace-notes.

In the XIXth. century, the writing of a Clementi, a Mendelssohn or a Chopin still often bears witness of such a tradition of pleasant volubility, and in the present day, although the taste for precise percussion and clear-cut rhythms seems to be in opposition to the development of a melodic curve revived from ancient formulae, the anti-harmonic tendencies of contemporary young composers nevertheless re-invest with an unexpected reality those virtues of pianistic technique, to which nearly a century of vertical music seemed to have dealt a decisive blow.

This shows the importance of the study whose elements

will be found in the following exercises.

Legato or staccato playing, portando or brilliant and distinct execution, evenness of finger touch or variety of tone created by diversity of attack, such are the many modes of expression which here come into being, and whose immediate application is to be found in the interpretation of the works of the principal composers mentioned above.

The execution of grace-note, arabesque and fioritura, on heavier key-boards, than those for which they were conceived does not fail to offer distinct difficulties even to most skilful fingers, and it is hardly necessary to add that all these melodic artifices which animate the music of the XVIIIth. century receive the greatest benefits from the work which we prescribe, as do also the repetition or substitution of the fingers.

Since the essential principle of technique studied in this first chapter is evenness of touch, care must be taken, according to the different conformations of the hand, to curve the fingers in such a way that they each strike the note on the same level. This is a "sine qua non" for equality in the propulsion of the hammers on the strings, and consequently for perfection in the relation of tone between notes played in melodic succession.

It will be well not to count on the apparent facility of the formulae contained in this chapter. In any case, their study will soon dissipate this illusion.

SERIES A

Tenuto Finger Exercises.

As the position of the fingers is the same for all the formulae in this series, as well as for the formation of any chords taken from the examples in the transferable reference table, we think it useless to repeat the fingering for each exercise. The right hand will always be placed thus : 1,2,3,4,5, the left 5,4,3,2,1.

EXERCISE No 1*a*. *(Mobility of fingers taken separately.)*

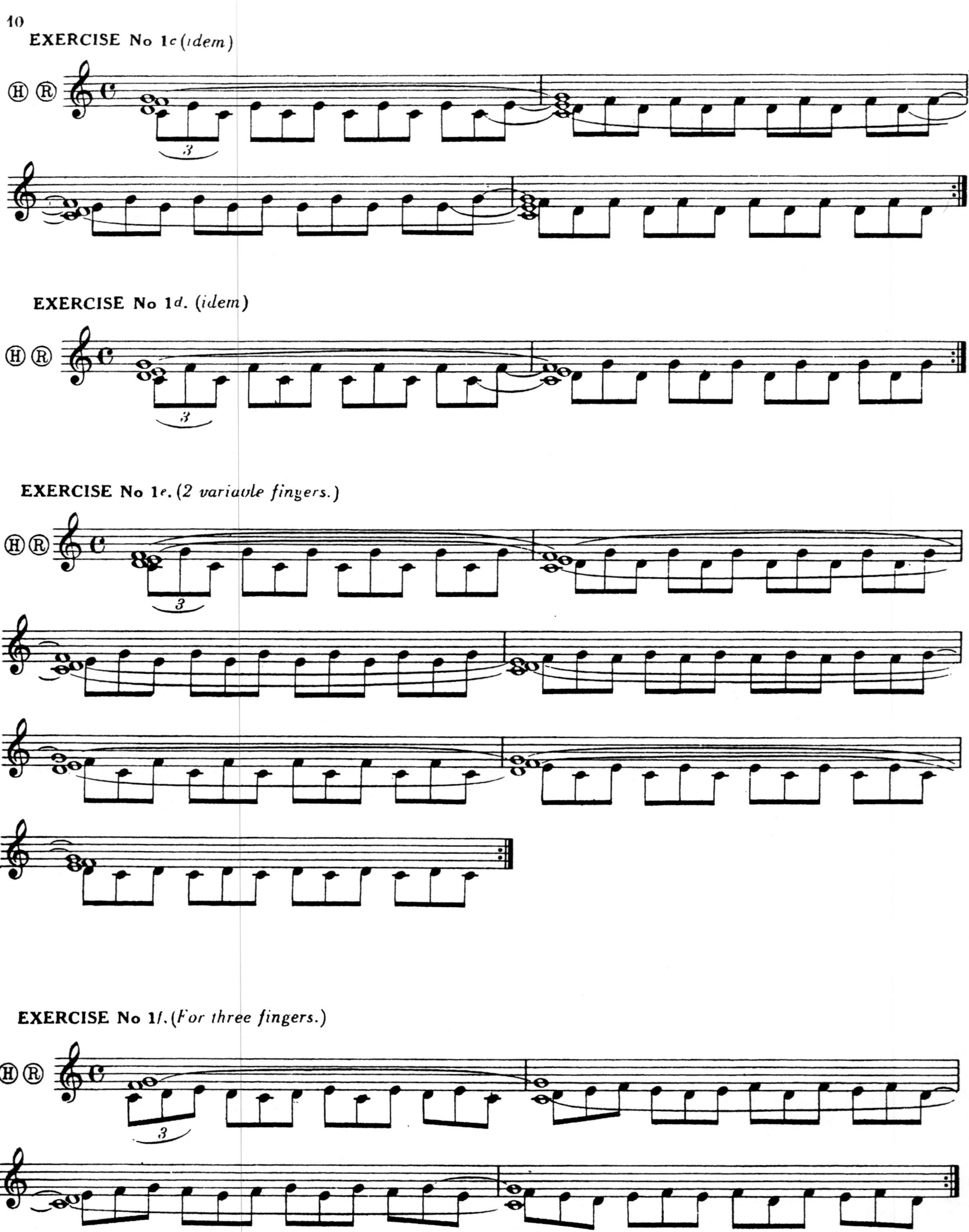
EXERCISE No 1c (idem)
Ⓗ Ⓡ
3
EXERCISE No 1d. (idem)
Ⓗ Ⓡ
3
EXERCISE No 1e. (2 variable fingers.)
Ⓗ Ⓡ
3
EXERCISE No 1f. (For three fingers.)
Ⓗ Ⓡ
3

EXERCISE No 1g. *(idem.)*

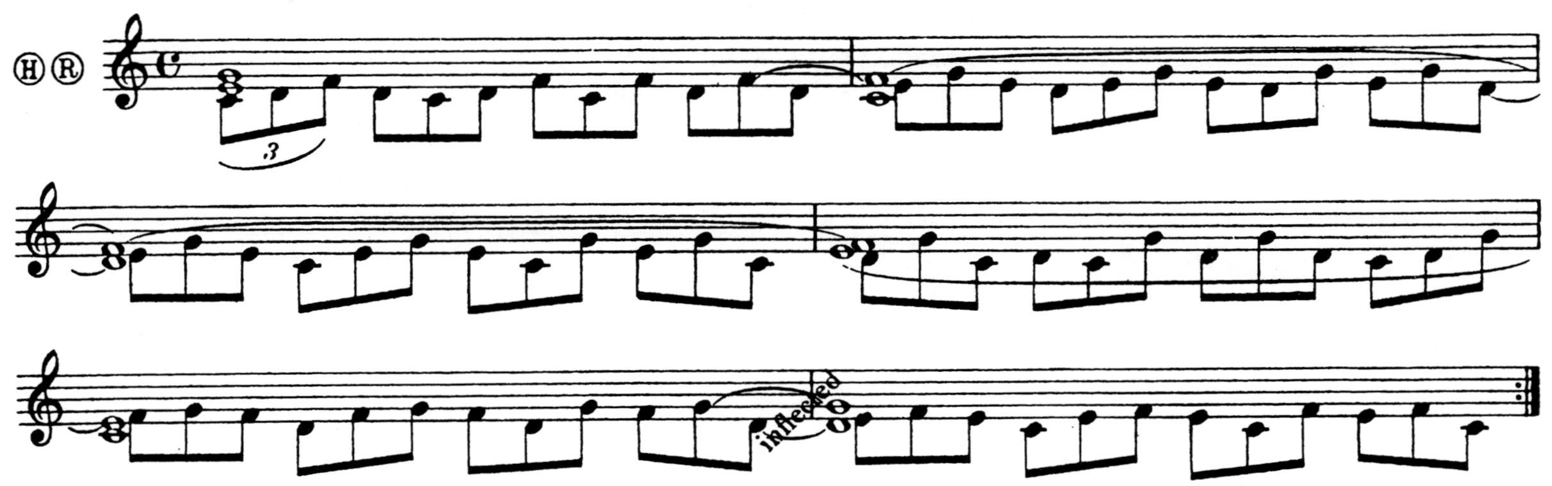

With the exception of the held notes which are always to be played *piano*, these exercises are to be practised alternately legato and in finger staccato, with conjunctive and percussive attack in the gradations *p*, *mf.* and *F* Metr=60 to 144 the crotchet.

Exercise for four fingers - With one finger held.

(Evenness and Independence of the Fingers)

The use of the held finger reduces any participation of the hand to a minimum in tone production, and while loosening the active fingers, favours their individual attack.

EXERCISE No 2a. *(Fingers held: r. h. thumb; l. h. 5th.)*

EXERCISE No 2b. *(Fingers held: r. h. 2nd; l. h. 4th.)*

EXERCISE No 2c. *(Fingers held: r. h. 3rd; l. h. 3rd.)*

EXERCISE No 2*d*. *(Fingers held: r. h. 4th; l. h. 2nd.)*

EXERCISE No 2*e*. *(Fingers held: r. h. 5th; l. h. thumb.)*

The semi-quavers are to be played alternately legato and staccato.

The use of the harmonic combinations in the transferable table will give rise to new disposals on the importance of whose study, no words can lay sufficient stress, this exercise being one of the most efficacious of this series.

SERIES B

Exercises with free fingers (without passing under of the Thumb)

EXERCISE No 1*a*. *(Beginning with the thumb r. h.; 5th. l. h.)*

EXERCISE No 1b. *(Beginning with the 2nd. finger r. h.; 4th. l. h.)*

EXERCISE No 1c. *(Beginning with the 3rd. finger of both hands)*

EXERCISE No 1d. *(Beginning with the 4th. finger r. h.; 2nd. l. h.)*

EXERCISE No 1c. *(Beginning with the 5th. finger r. h.; thumb l. h.)*

As we have pointed out in the plan of study, we recall the fact that the sign (C) implies the daily chromatic transposition in immediate succession of the formulae contained between the double bar and the repeat. The study of Exercise No. 1*a.* which we give here by way of example, will therefore present itself in the following form :

The same will be observed for all the following formulae, and will in no way affect the harmonic and rhythmic modifications brought about by the use of the variants given in the table and referred to by the signs (H) and (R).

We also advise that all the formulae should be linked together in a different key each day, contrasting the degrees of rapidity and the dynamics, the fingers playing alternately legato and staccato. In this last case the repetition of each note with the same finger will give the best of results.

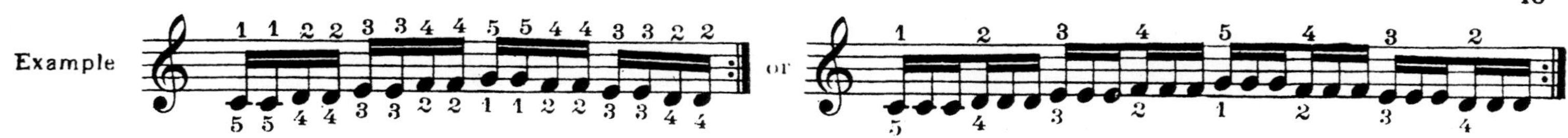

See that the fingers not in action are absolutely relaxed. all the effort being centred on the finger in action.

EXERCISE No 2a. *(Evenness of the fingers in a succession of different rhythms.)*

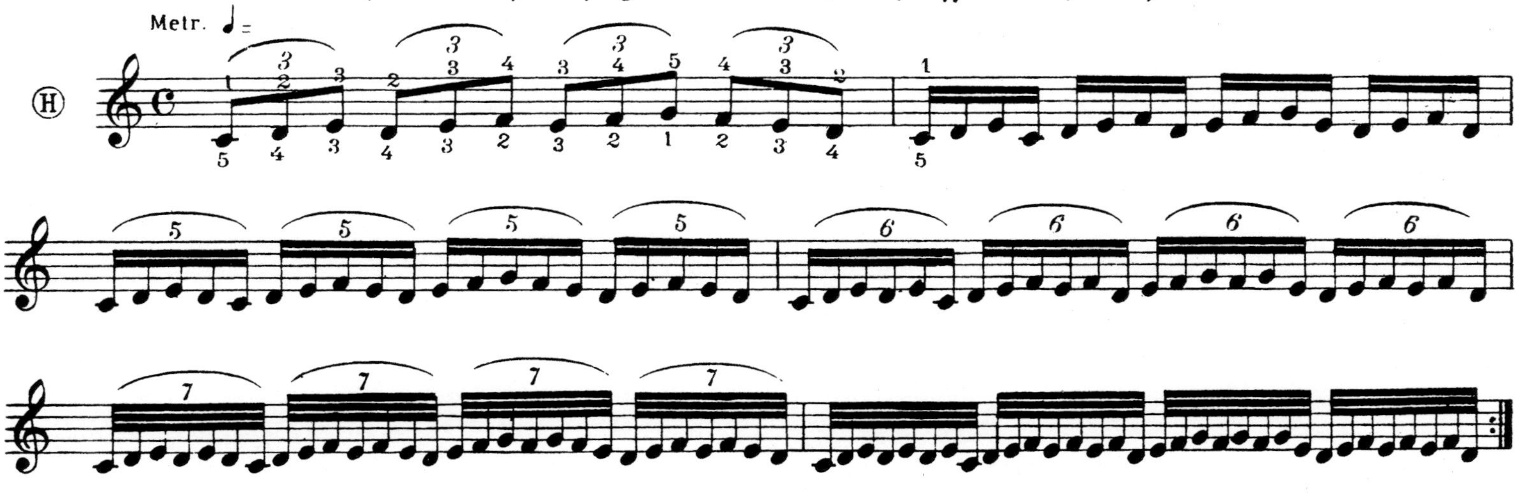

Metr. ♩=

EXERCISE No 2b.

EXERCISE No 2c.

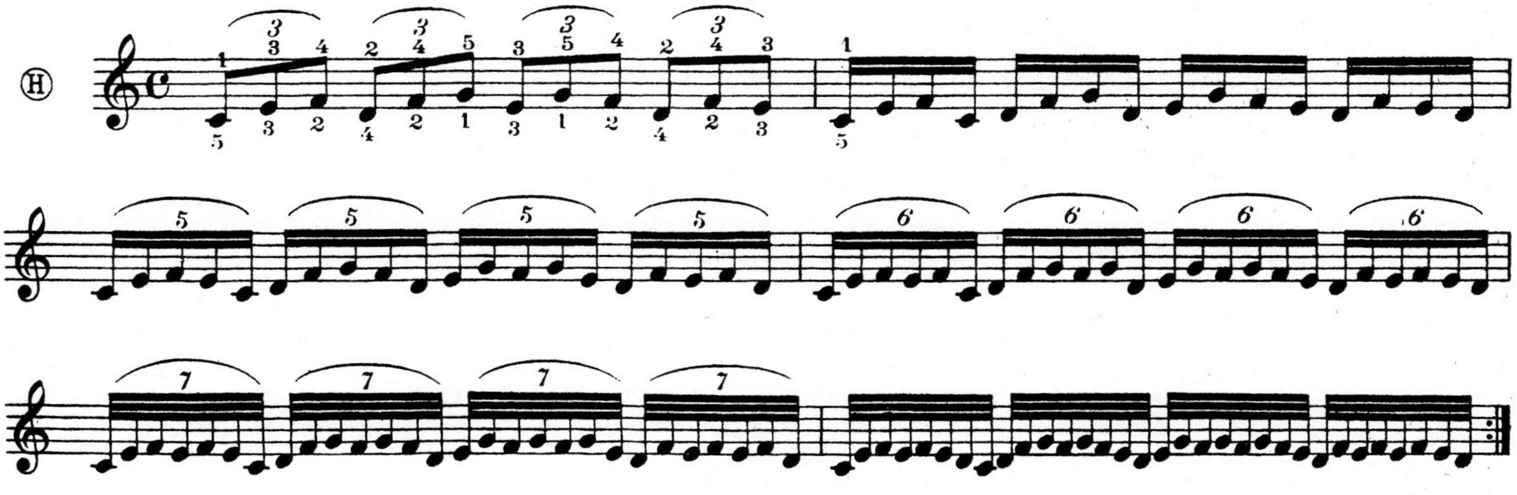

EXERCISE No 2*d*.

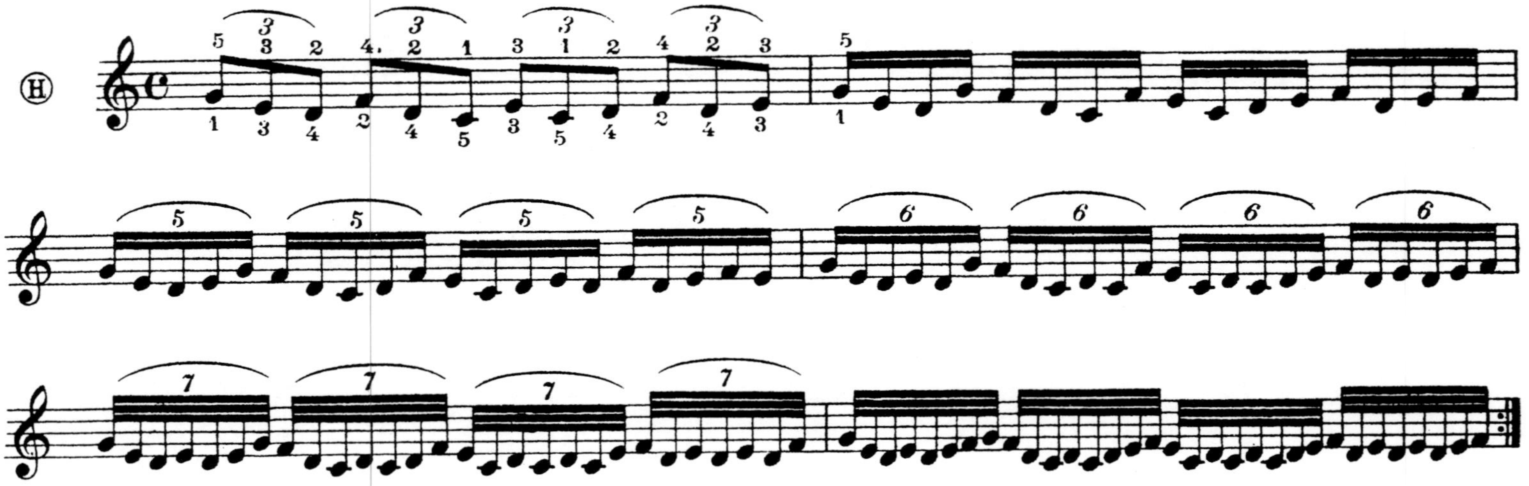

EXERCISE No 2*e*.

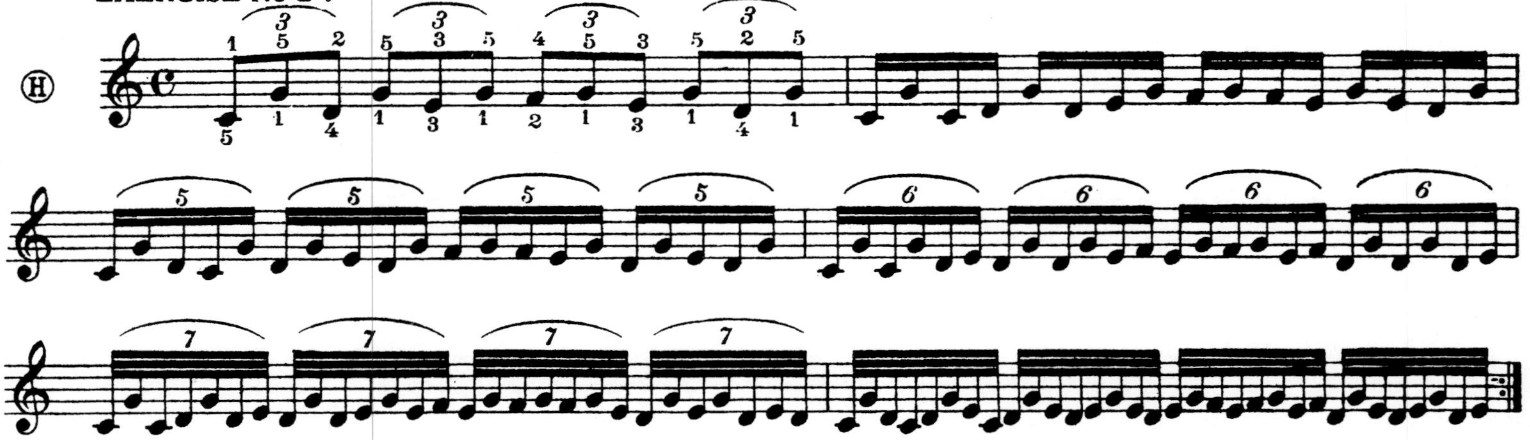

EXERCISE No 2*f*.

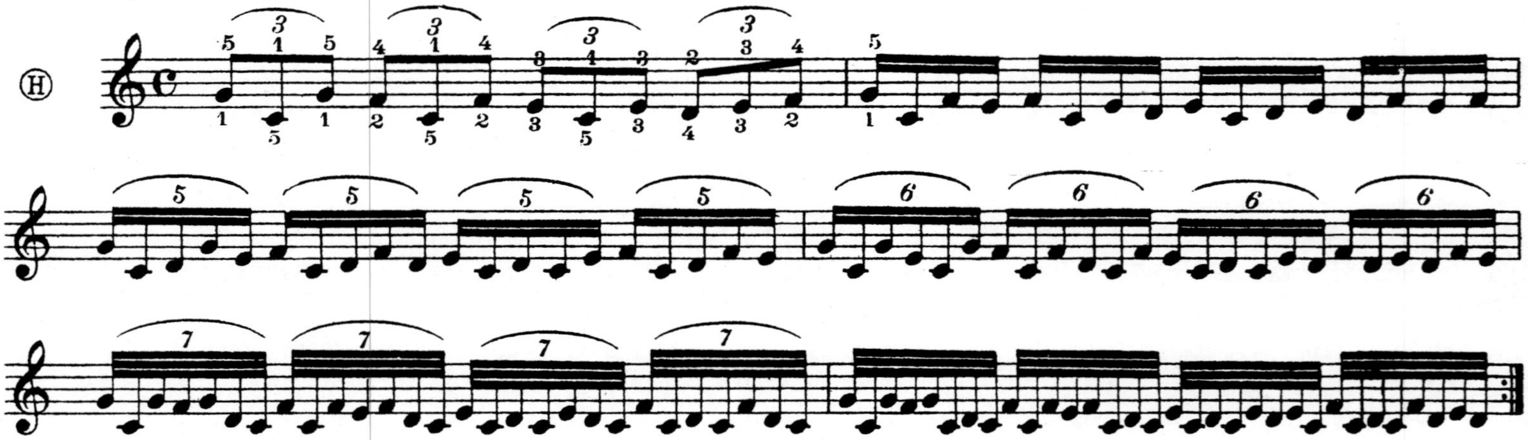

For the study of these exercises in contrary motion for both hands, we recall the fact that since the position of the fingers on the keys is invariable the left hand need only play using the fingering marked for the right hand and vice versa.

Examples

The same fingering

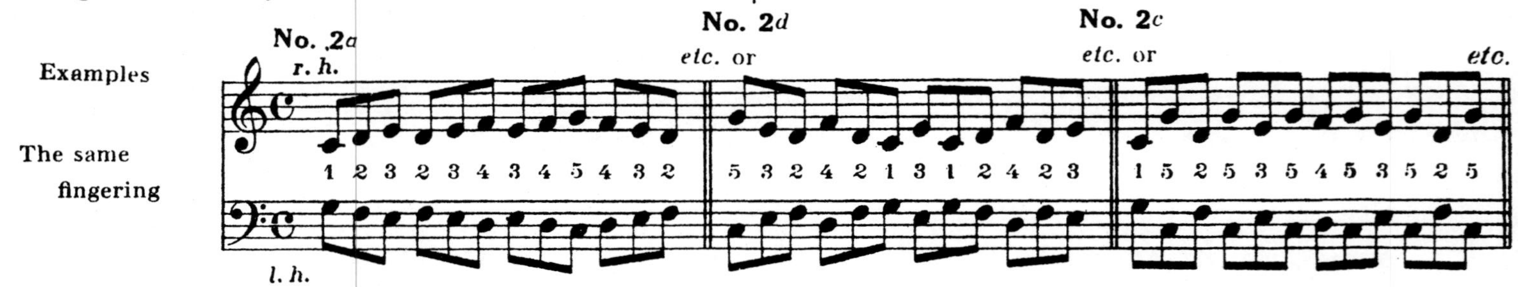

All the exercises in Series B can also be practised with hands crossed, the left hand playing an octave above the right hand, sometimes passing over it, and sometimes under.

EXERCISE No 1a. (Lateral finger movements, conjunct motion.)
r. h.
l. h.
EXERCISE No 1b. (Idem. Disjunct motion.)
EXERCISE No 2. (Sliding the same finger chromatically.)
EXERCISE No 3a. (Change of finger on the same key.)
simile
simile
simile
simile
EXERCISE No 3b. (Idem. With one finger held.)

EXERCISE No 3c. (*Idem. With two fingers held.*)

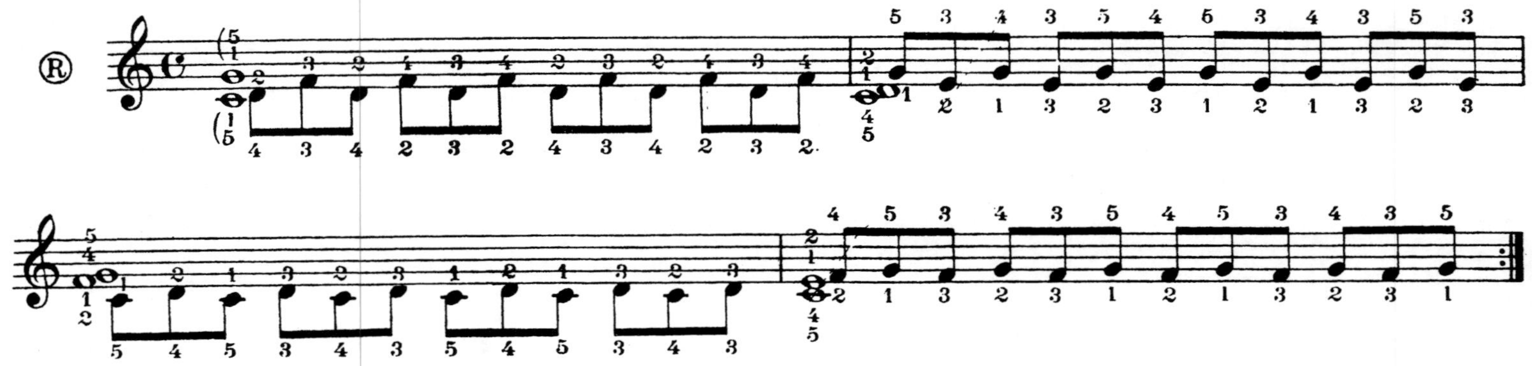

EXERCISE No 4a. (*Diatonic crossing of fingers.*)

EXERCISE No 4b. (*Chromatic crossing of fingers.*)

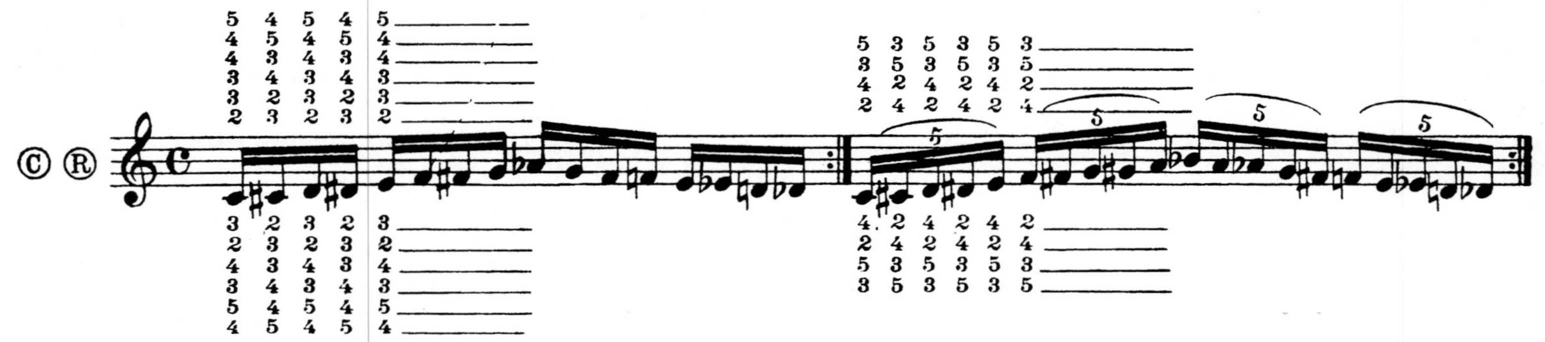

Also to be practised with the fingering 2 3 4, 2 4 3, 2 3 4 5, 2 4 3 5, *etc.*

EXERCISE No 5a. *Legato substitution of fingers. (Slide the fingers successively on to the same key without sounding it.)*

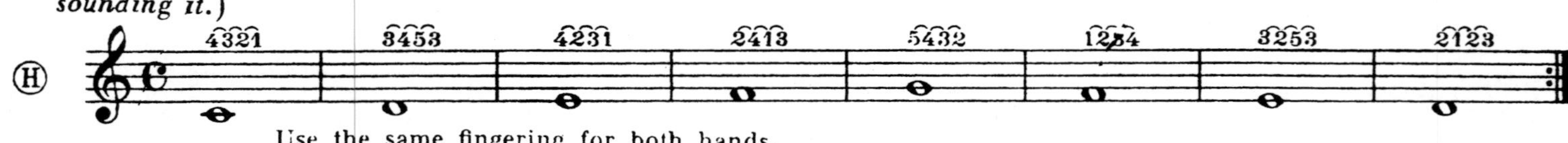

Use the same fingering for both hands.

EXERCISE No 5b. (*Articulate substitution of the fingers on the same key.*)

EXERCISE No 6a. *Repetition of the same note with different fingers (two fingers.)*

EXERCISE No 6b. *Idem. (For 3 fingers.)*

EXERCISE No 6c. *Idem. (For 4 fingers.)*

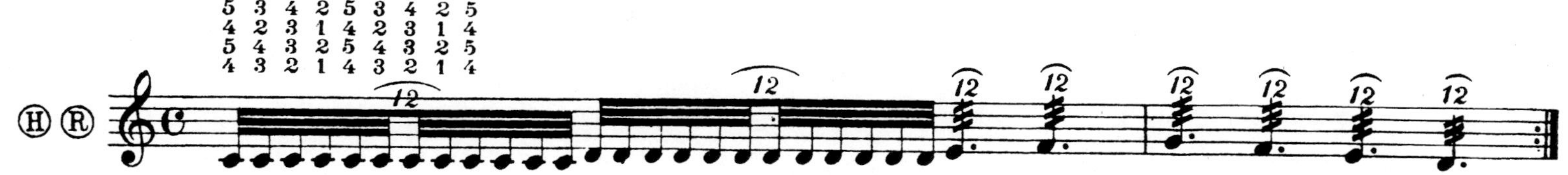

EXERCISE No 6d. *Idem. (For 5 fingers.)*

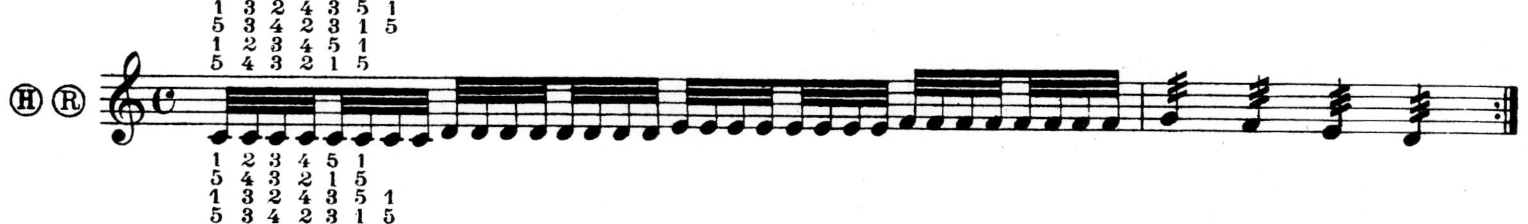

EXERCISE No 7a. *(Shakes and double shakes.)*

EXERCISE No 7b. *(Grupetti with upward termination.)*

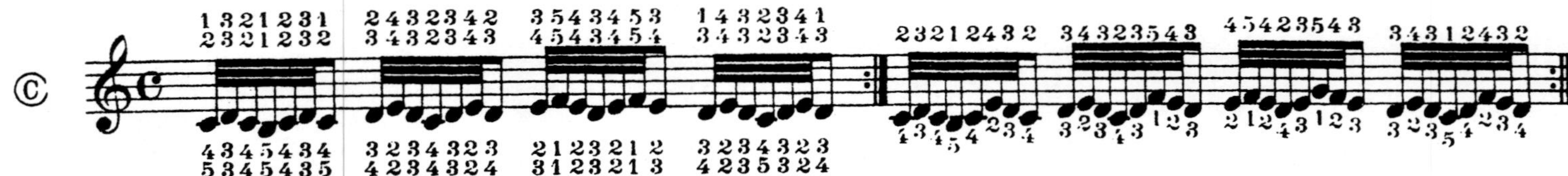

EXERCISE No 7c. *(Grupetti with downward termination.)*

EXERCISE No 8a. *(Trills.)*

To be practised in all positions with a new fingering for each bar. In spite of the similarity of the last bar of this Exercise with No. 3a, of Series C, it will be necessary to devote fresh study to it here.

EXERCISE No 8b. *(Trills with held fingers.)*

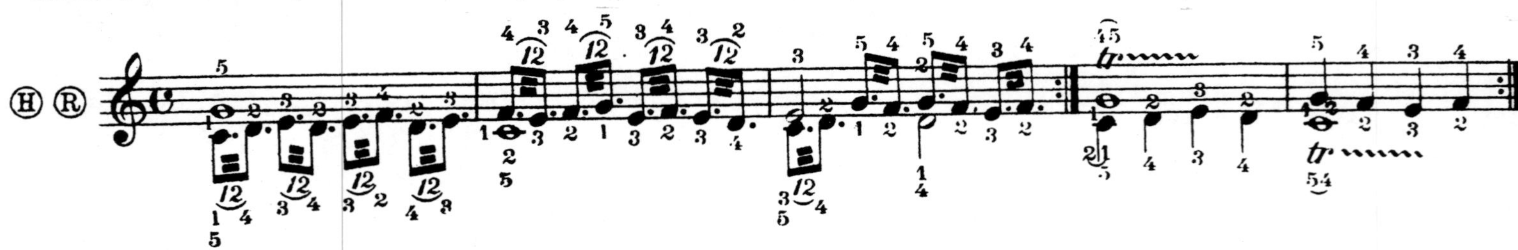

EXERCISE No 8c. *(Linked trills.)*

(to be continued on further melodic formulae.)

The exercises contained in this first chapter are equally suitable to both kinds of hand, whose characteristics we have defined by denominating them hands with long or with short fingers.

For the latter it is, however, advisable to avoid prolonged study of the formulae with held fingers, and it will be found advantageous to alternate the exercises of Series A & B daily.

It will bring forth better results to study most of Series B legato rather than staccato.

Complementary Formulae for Exercises

Composed by the Pupil or Recommended by the Teacher

Nota.—Father Mersenne, in his treatise on «Universal Harmony» estimates the number of musical combinations which can be established on five different notes at 150.

We leave to the imagination of the pupil the vertiginous figure to which the new formulae might amount in the work of invention in which we here invite him to exercise nis ingenuity.

CHAPTER II

Passing under of the thumb - Scales - Arpeggios

We have elsewhere laid stress (see the Students' Edition of Chopin's Studies — commentary N° 8 op. 10) on the importance of the part played by the thumb in the technique of the pianoforte, and indicated some formulae for exercises capable of developing suppleness and lightness in the movements of this member.

An amplification of these exercises will be found in this chapter. Experience has given us proof of the efficacity of this mode of work, and we particularly recommend it.

We think that it would not be out of place, at the beginning of this special study, to give a brief outline of the history of that principle of fingering, which shows the chief difference between the school of the pianoforte, and that of the harpsichord. It has only been generally adopted at a relatively recent date — hardly 150 years ago — and corresponds to a completely new departure in virtuosity, and as a natural reaction, in musical invention.

It is well known that up to the end of the XVIIth century the use of the thumb on key-board instruments was, if not forbidden, at any rate totally neglected.

Performers contented themselves with only using the four fingers, which found their place most naturally on the keys. This, perhaps for aesthetic reasons, and also because of the melodic requirements of the period, the restrained choice of tonalities, and the limited dimensions of the instruments, which did not entail a very wide range of displacements for the hand. The thumb was either allowed to trail carelessly beneath the hand, or to lean on the outer casing of the key-board.

Ascending and descending progressions were obtained by passing the fingers across one another, a proceeding which seems never to have been submitted to any precise rule. Apparently, however, the combination employed for preference, was the crossing over of the second and third fingers.

Even in Purcell's and Couperin's time, in the most glorious epoch of the art of the harpsichord, the use of the thumb is only occasional, and almost exclusively limited to the first note of a scale. After that, it is very rarely designated in a melodic formula, if we judge by the few indications for fingering handed down to us in the editions of the period.

It is to John Sebastian Bach that we are indebted not only for the " Well tempered Clavichord ", that is, the clavichord or harpischord equivalently tuned to suit all the different keys, but also, it seems, for the " well fingered clavichord ", just as his key-board writing has a greater wealth and loftiness of style than that of his French or Italian rivals, so it bespoke a very special virtuosity, for which the use of all the fingers was not too much .

It is in the interpretation of his works, that we shall learn, for the lucid translation of frequently juxtaposed melodic designs, the use of the thumb in every key and in almost every position.

It fell to the lot of his illustrious son, Charles-Philip-Emmanuel Bach, to systematize, to a certain extent, the new principles of fingering, and to introduce the regular use of passing the thumb under in scales, thus preparing the way for the technique of Mozart and of Haydn.

He still makes numerous reservations for the legitimacy of this procedure, in certain cases, and he subordinates it to considerations of musical expediency, rather than technical convenience. Towards the year 1800, Clementi gives precision and generality to the innovations of his predecessors, in his admirable " Gradus ad Parnassum ". In reality, it is only dating from his time that the custom is established, of employing the thumb methodically, twice in the octave, in the course of a scale, and of using it as a pivot to enable the hand to travel over several octaves, by means of arpeggios or composite figures.

It is by an evident coincidence that we see, from this period onwards, a richer and more comprehensive pianistic style now become almost dramatic, aiming no longer at merely copying the naïve artifices of the singer, but at equalling the expressive power of the orchestra.

That the substitution, in musical practice, of the timbre of the piano, for that of the harpsichord, and the extension of the key-board, both in the treble and the bass, should have been sufficient cause, apart from any purely aesthetic consideration, to bring about the radical change in character which we notice in the composers of the end of the XVIIIth century, are facts too obvious for further demonstration.

But for the complete expression of a new element of tonal inspiration, the support of an appropriate technique became necessary.

We think that we are not mistaken in looking upon the universally admitted use of passing the thumb, that means of multiplying the fingers, that eminent factor of velocity, father of octaviation, as the essential technical principle in the veritable revolution which, in less than 40 years, overthrew all the conventions of pianistic writing, rising to a climax in the magnificent instrumental audacities, of a Lizst or of a Thalberg.

SERIES A

Mobility of the thumb (scales and arpeggios)

EXERCISE No 1a. (*lateral and detached movements of thumb with the hand remaining motionless and the finger held.*)

(same fingering for both hands)

(for long-fingered hands only)

(for long-fingered hands only)

EXERCISE No 1b. (*idem with several fingers held.*)

EXERCISE No 1c. (*idem legato movements of the thumb.*

EXERCISE No 1d.

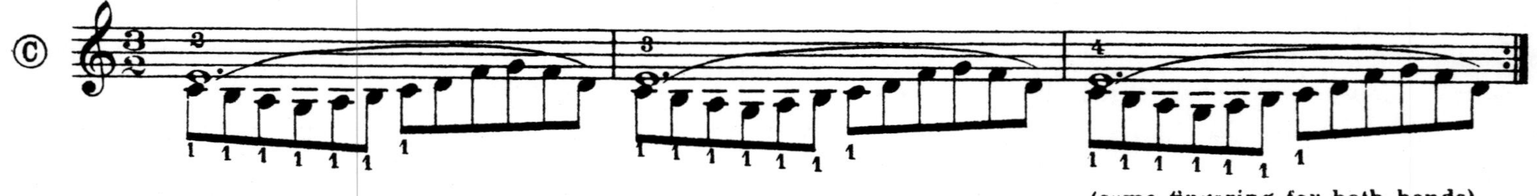

(same fingering for both hands)

EXERCISE No 2a. (*idem, hand in motion with finger held.*)

same fingering for both hands. Employ the 2nd, 3rd, and 4th fingers successively, for the held notes.

EXERCISE No 2b. (*idem.*)

to be practised in the same way as exercise No 2a.

EXERCISE No 3a. *(idem.)*

(same fingering for both hands)

EXERCISE No 3b. *(idem, two fingers held.)*

simile

EXERCISE No 3c. *(chromatic progression.)*

EXERCISE No 4. *(for the lightness in thumb transmission.)*

r. h. l. h.

SERIES B

Study of scales and arpeggios

The action of the thumb in scales and arpeggios, as an agent for the multiplication of the fingers, should neither cause any inequality of tone, any modification in the position of the other fingers, nor any diminution of speed in rapid playing.

For the ideal execution of the legato scale, we suggest the following notation in which the upper line shows the mute position of the fingers on the keys, the lower line, the notes actually played.

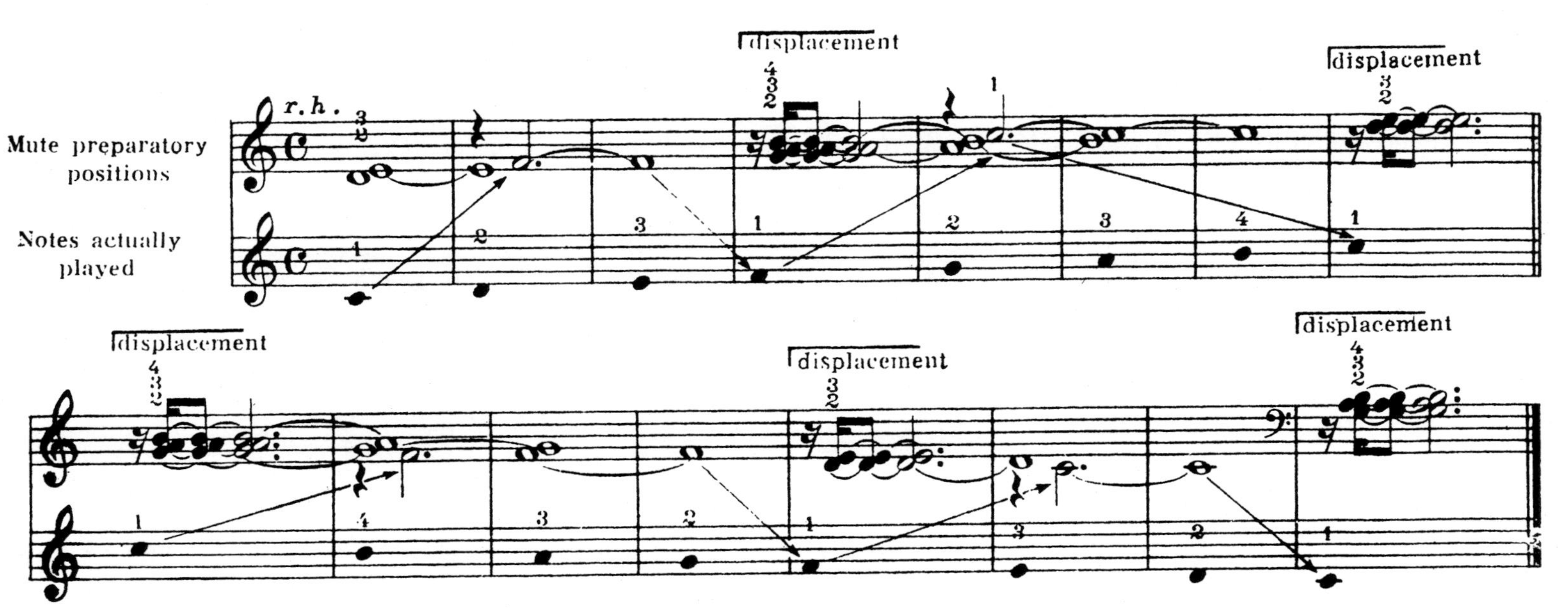

The left hand is also to be practised from this example. It will be noticed that according to the anatomical conformation of the hand and its adaptation to the keyboard, the passing under of the thumb necessitates a different mechanism when produced in ascending motion, to that demanded for descending motion. Its execution is less easy in the ascent of the right hand, and in the descent of the left. Its perfect smoothness in both cases is obtained by the preparation of the thumb's attack and by rapid lateral displacement of the hand.

EXERCISE No 1*a*. (*preparation of the attack of the thumb.*)

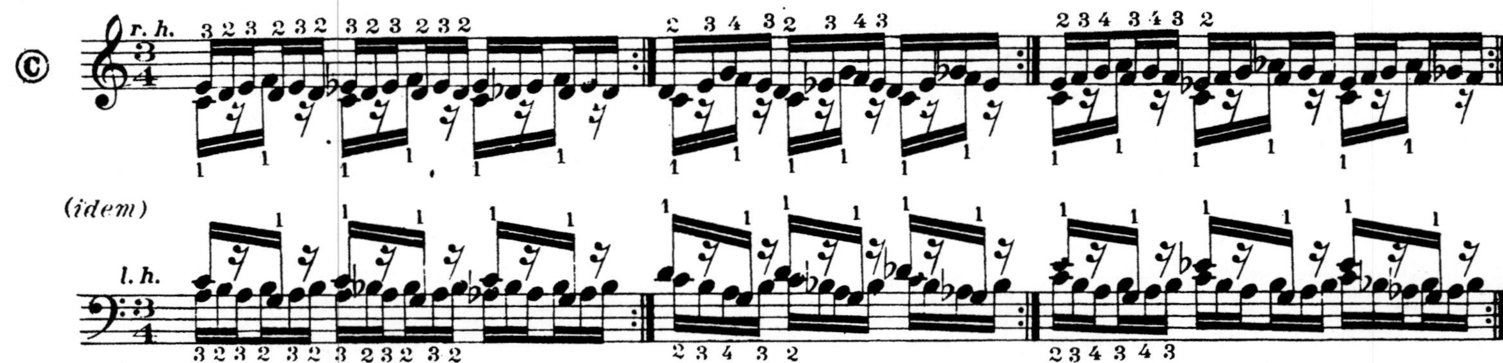

Slide the thumb very close to the key-board, approaching the note it will have to strike, as soon as possible. Reduce all participation of the hand in this movement, to a minimum, which will be facilited by a slight flexion of the wrist.

EXERCISE No 2*a*. (*Displacement of the hand. the thumb remaining motionless.*)

EXERCISE No 2*b*. (*idem.*)

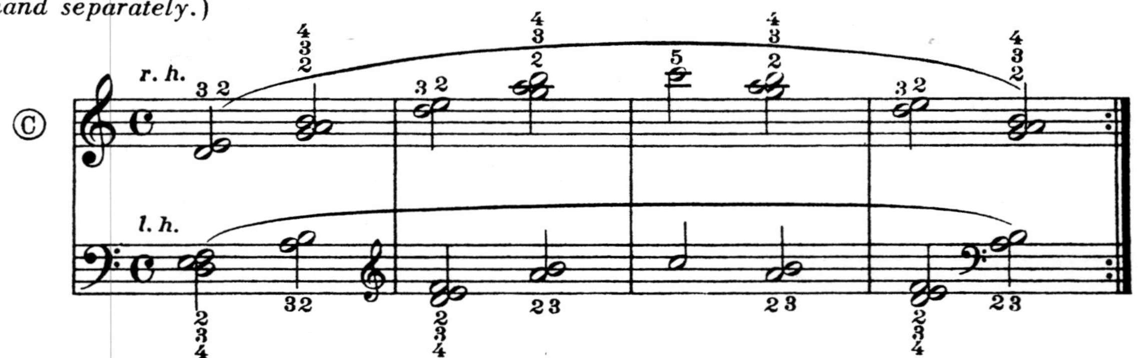

EXERCISE No 3*a*. (*ascending and descending displacements of the hand, without using the thumb. Practise each hand separately.*)

In this exercise the hand will make its lateral advance by closely skimming the key-board.

EXERCISE No 3*b*. (*idem; let the thumb play lightly; practise each hand separately.*)

In this last exercise the thumb must only give the gentlest touch to the keys and immediately slip under the other fingers, into position for its next attack. See that the crotchets are sounded absolutely simultaneously.

EXERCISE No 4a. *(rapidity of the passing under of the thumb, combined with all the fingers. The same fingering for both hands.)*

Make the pause on the minims quite distinct, and play the small notes very lightly.

EXERCISE No 4b. *(mixed fingerings.)*

EXERCISE No 5.

A. *Scales for 3 fingers in all keys*

B. *Scales for 4 fingers*

C. *Scales for 5 fingers*

Start with the thumb on every note of the scale in turn. Employ the following mixed successions of fingers also, thus : 1 2 1 2 3, 1 2 1 2 3 4, 1 2 1 2 3 4 5, 1 2 3 1 2 3 4, 1 2 3 1 2 3 4 5, as well as the combinations shown on the transferable table.

EXERCISE No 6. *(For this exercise study a scale in a different key each day, using the traditional fingering, in unison, in thirds, in sixths, in tenths, in contrary motion, with crossed hands, varying the movement, shading, and rhythms, and play alternately legato and staccato.)*

ARPEGGIOS. The mechanism for passing the thumb under, in the execution of arpeggios requires a slightly more accentuated flexion of the wrist than for scales, in proportion to the stretch imposed upon the fingers preparing the return of the hand to its normal position.

(Notation of the ideal position of the fingers for the execution of arpeggios.)

EXERCISE No 7a. *(preparation for the attack of the thumb : practise each hand separately.)*

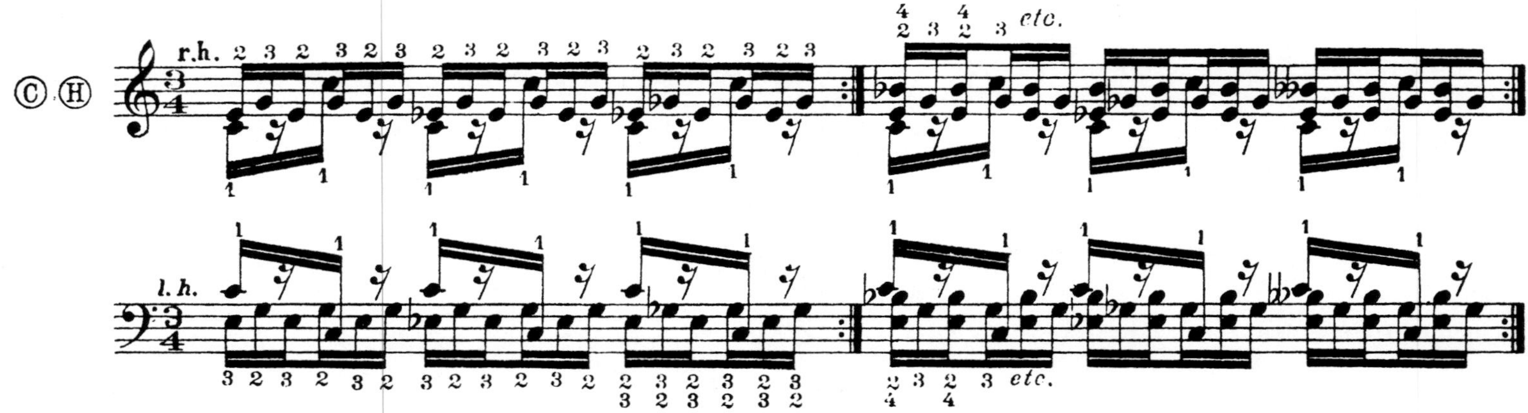

EXERCISE No 7b *(displacement of the hand. the thumb remaining motionless.)*

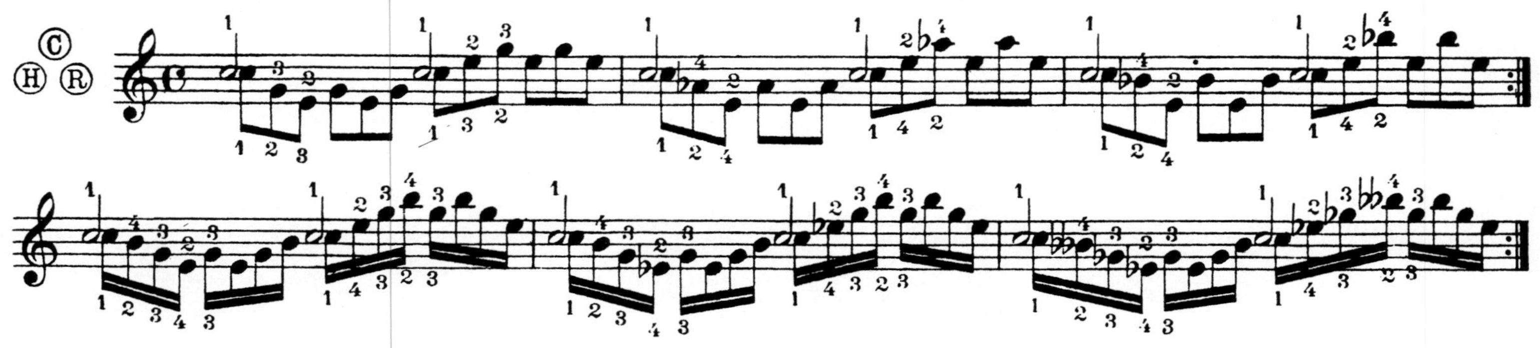

EXERCISE No 8. *idem; delicate use of the thumb (see note : Exercise No. 3b.)*

EXERCISE No 9a. *(rapidity of the thumb combined with all the fingers.)*

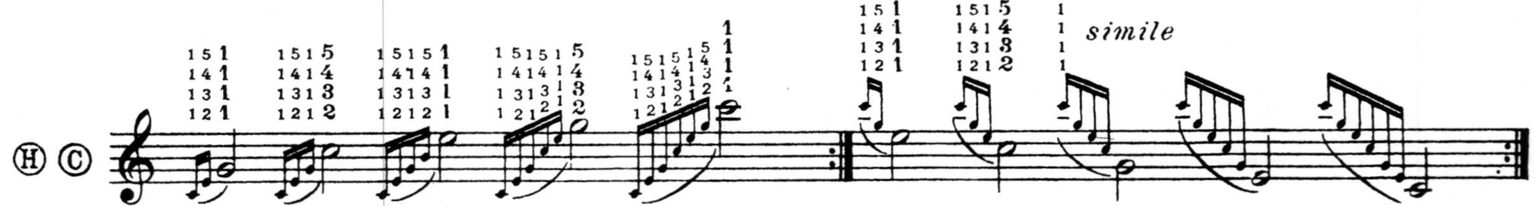

Same fingering for both hands. Make a distinct pause on the minims. Play the small notes lightly.

EXERCISE No 9b. *(mixed fingerings.)*

EXERCISE No 10*a*.

A. (*arpeggios for 3 fingers on perfect chords.*)

B. (*arpeggios for 4 fingers, idem.*)

C. (*arpeggios for 5 fingers, idem.*)

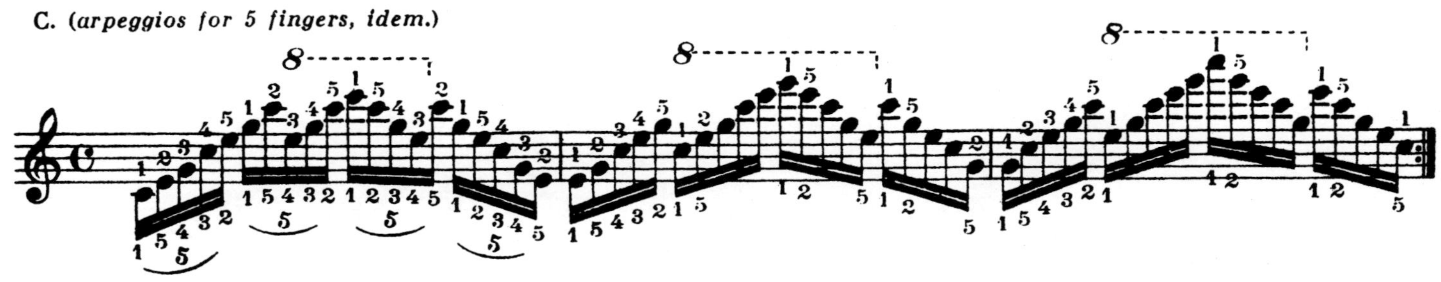

EXERCISE No 10*b*.

A. (*arpeggios for 3 fingers on the chords of the seventh.*)

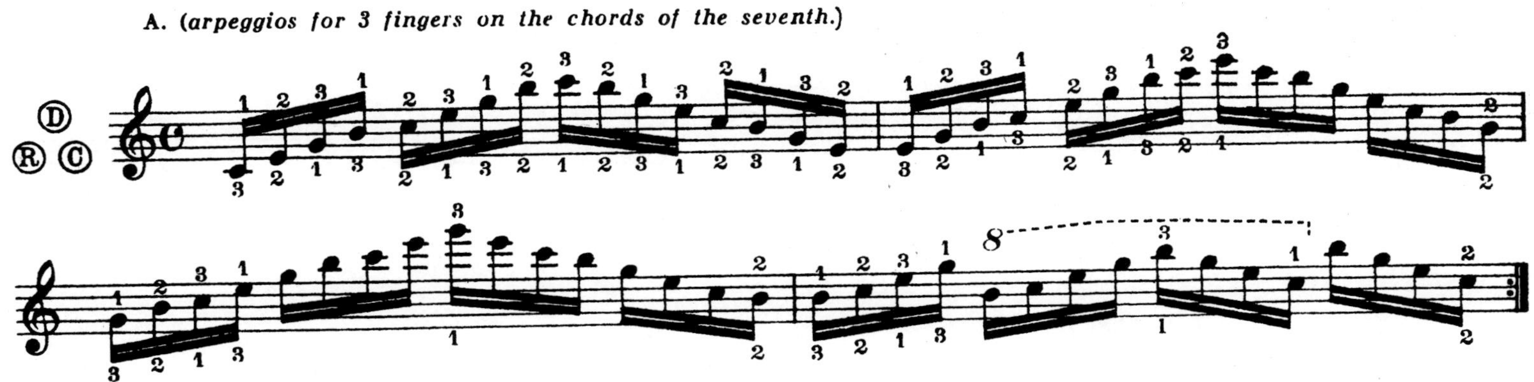

b) Arpeggios for 4 fingers : same positions. Employ the succession 1234 for the right hand; 4321 for the left.

c) Arpeggios for 5 fingers : same positions. Employ the succession 12345 for the right hand; 54321 for the left.

Also use the mixed fingerings shown Exercise N° 5.

EXERCISE No 11 *This exercise will comprise the daily study of an arpeggio with its usual fingering, in all positions, inversions, etc. in a new key each day. For this study, conform to the indications given above for exercise N° 6 alternating arpeggios on perfect chords with arpeggios of the seventh of all kinds.*

SERIES C

The chromatic scale - Broken chords
Composite figures

The chromatic scale.

(In our plan of work, we purposely reserve a place, between the study of arpeggios and that of broken chords, for the study of the chromatic scale, so as to counteract the muscular effort caused by the technique of wide stretches, by the relaxation of a compact position of the hand.)

EXERCISE No 1*a.* *(preparation for the chromatic scale, the* **passing under** *of the thumb in opposition to all fingers)*

the same fingering for both hands.

EXERCISE No 1*b.* *(fingering for 3 fingers.)*

EXERCISE No 1*c.* *(fingering for 4 fingers.)*

EXERCISE No 1*d.* *(fingering for 5 fingers.)*

The object of opposing the rhythms to their respective fingerings in these exercises is to avoid the accentuation of the thumb which counteracts even playing.

EXERCISE No 2. *In this exercise the chromatic scale will be studied in conformity with the preceding indication for exercise N° 6, Series B. of this chapter. Henceforward the three fingerings most frequently used will be found, together with the designation of the kinds of execution to which they are most applicable.*

(1) brio, firmness — (2) lightness, rapidity — (3) without the thumb, extreme softness, legato.

Broken chords.

A broken chord is nothing but a formation of arpeggios, in which the regular succession of the notes is inverted. The fingering is, in most cases determined by considerations of rhythmic punctuation, which render the position of the thumb liable to every kind of modification. The examples below are established in view of these modifications. That is to say they are subject to variation brought about by the use of the rhythms, fingerings and harmonic formations in the transferable table. Each note in these formations can be used as a starting point for a new exercise established on the pattern of the following formulae :

EXERCISE No 3. *(elementary formulae and traditional fingerings of broken chords.)*

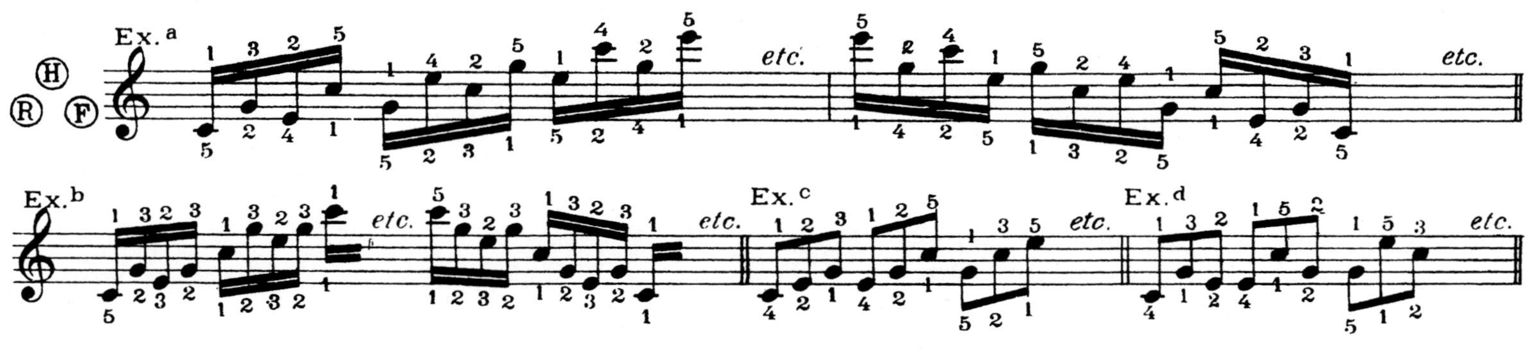

VARIANTS *broken chords of 3 sounds.*

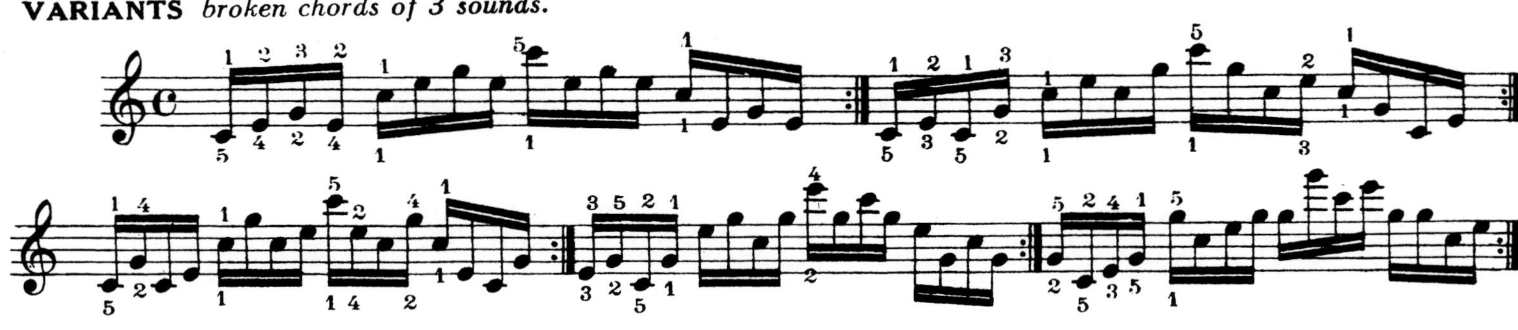

broken chords of 4 sounds.

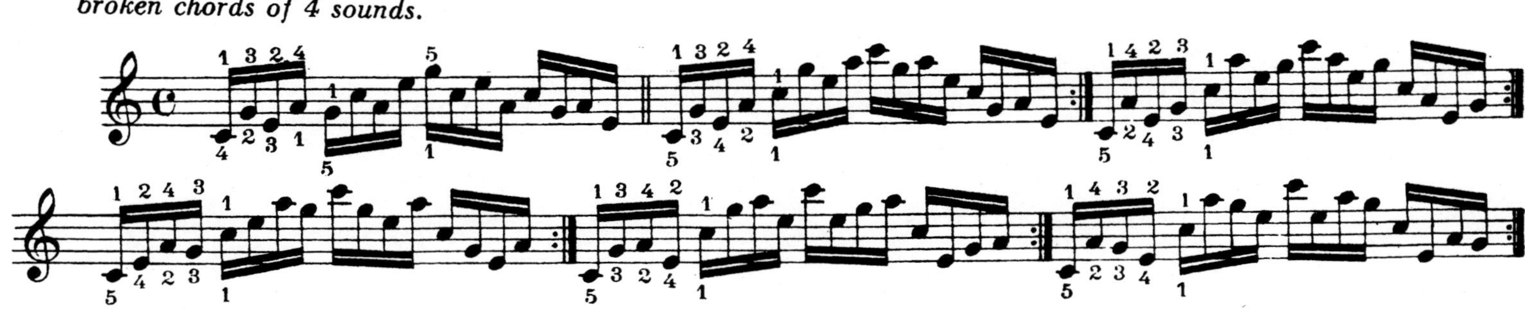

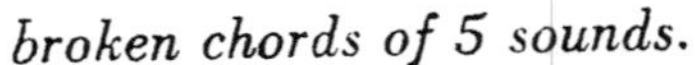

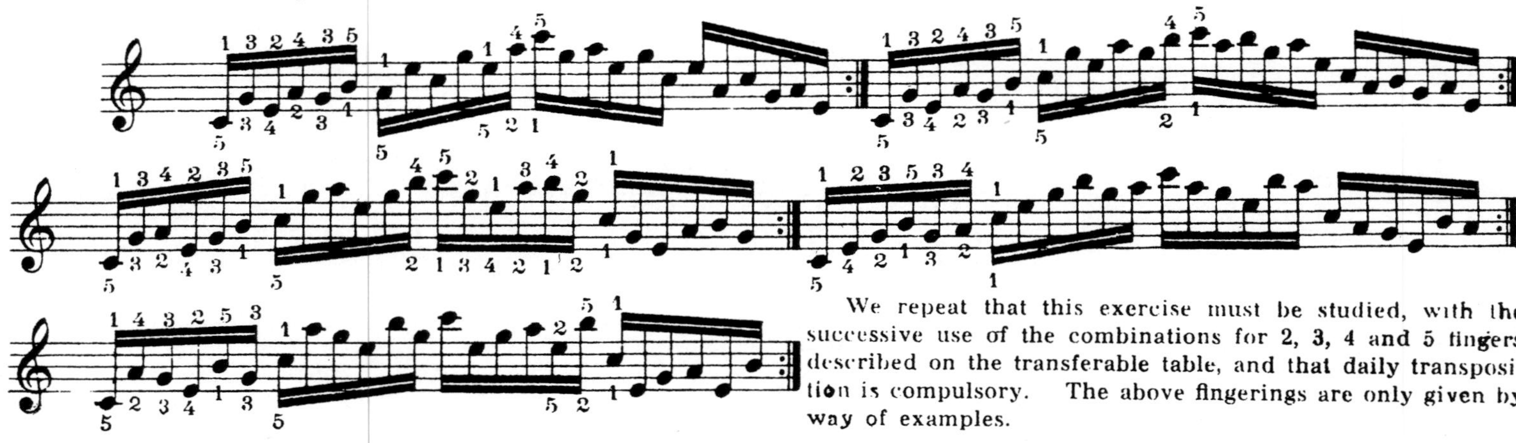

We repeat that this exercise must be studied, with the successive use of the combinations for 2, 3, 4 and 5 fingers described on the transferable table, and that daily transposition is compulsory. The above fingerings are only given by way of examples.

Models of complementary exercises of chromatic formation, with variable fingerings.

(Thumb transmission in composite figures.)

By the denomination composite figures, we mean the grouping together, in a single melodic formula, generally of a brilliant or rapid nature, and usually consisting of a succession of notes of equal value, of two elements, which for the Monsieur Jourdain (1) of to day suffice for the construction of all music. We are speaking of conjunct and disjunct motion, or let us say, for the sake of simplicity : scales and arpeggios.

We shall not enter — and with reason — into the unlimited complications to which this mixture can give rise.

Although each epoch has marked this form of virtuosity with its own particular character and accent, yet have several centuries of musical writing not visibly reduced its endless possibilities of renewal.

We shall limit ourselves to the proposal of examples for daily practice, based on what may be termed the scheme governing the systematic opposition of these two movements. We shall leave the further pursuit of this study, by the preparation of works, the very basis of whose composition is provided by this special technique, to the zeal of the pupil, and to the judicious initiative of the teacher. The reader will find, at the end of this volume, a summary list of these works, given merely by way of an indication for the direction of research.

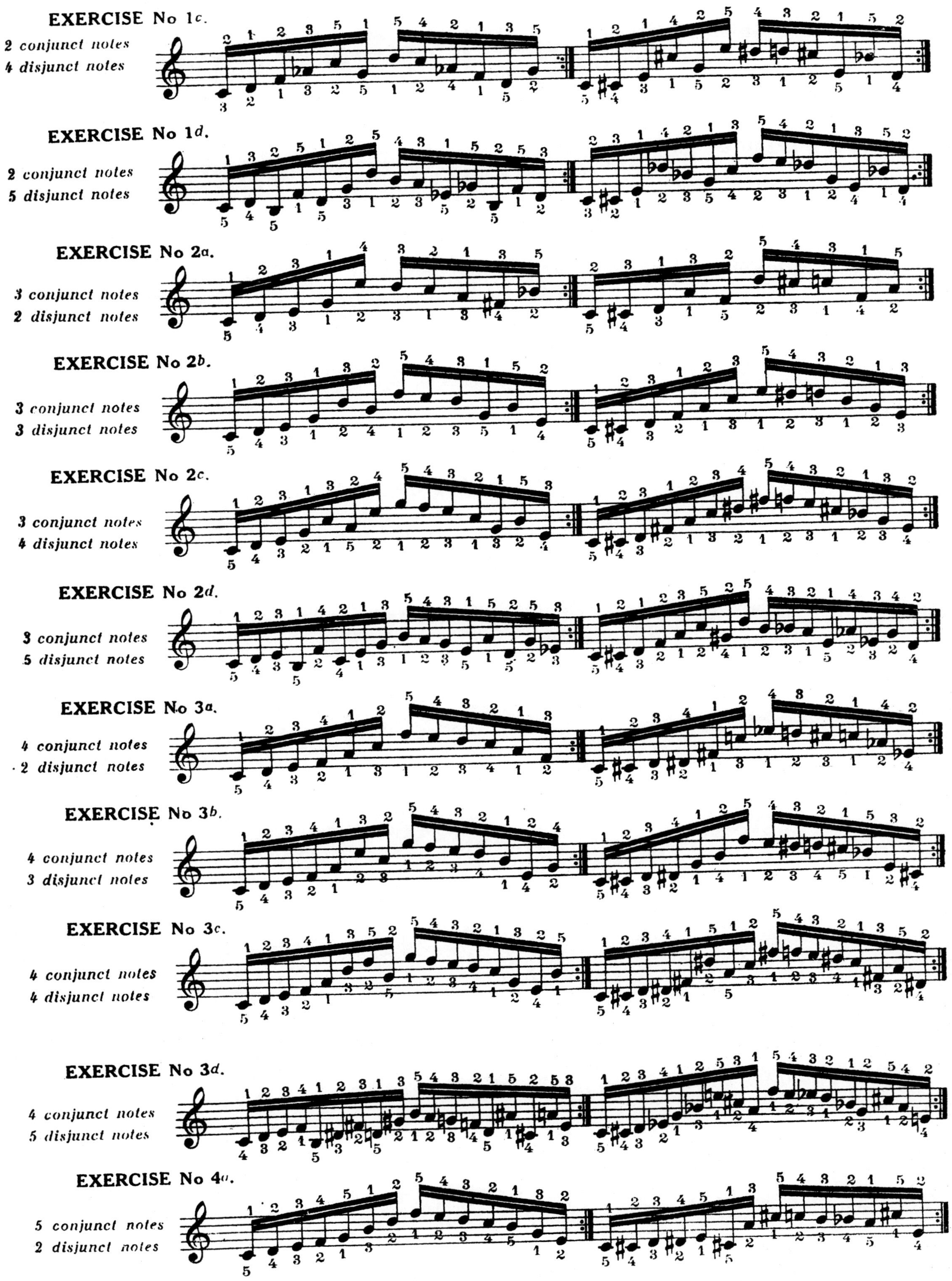
EXERCISE No 1c.
2 conjunct notes
4 disjunct notes
EXERCISE No 1d.
2 conjunct notes
5 disjunct notes
EXERCISE No 2a.
3 conjunct notes
2 disjunct notes
EXERCISE No 2b.
3 conjunct notes
3 disjunct notes
EXERCISE No 2c.
3 conjunct notes
4 disjunct notes
EXERCISE No 2d.
3 conjunct notes
5 disjunct notes
EXERCISE No 3a.
4 conjunct notes
2 disjunct notes
EXERCISE No 3b.
4 conjunct notes
3 disjunct notes
EXERCISE No 3c.
4 conjunct notes
4 disjunct notes
EXERCISE No 3d.
4 conjunct notes
5 disjunct notes
EXERCISE No 4a.
5 conjunct notes
2 disjunct notes

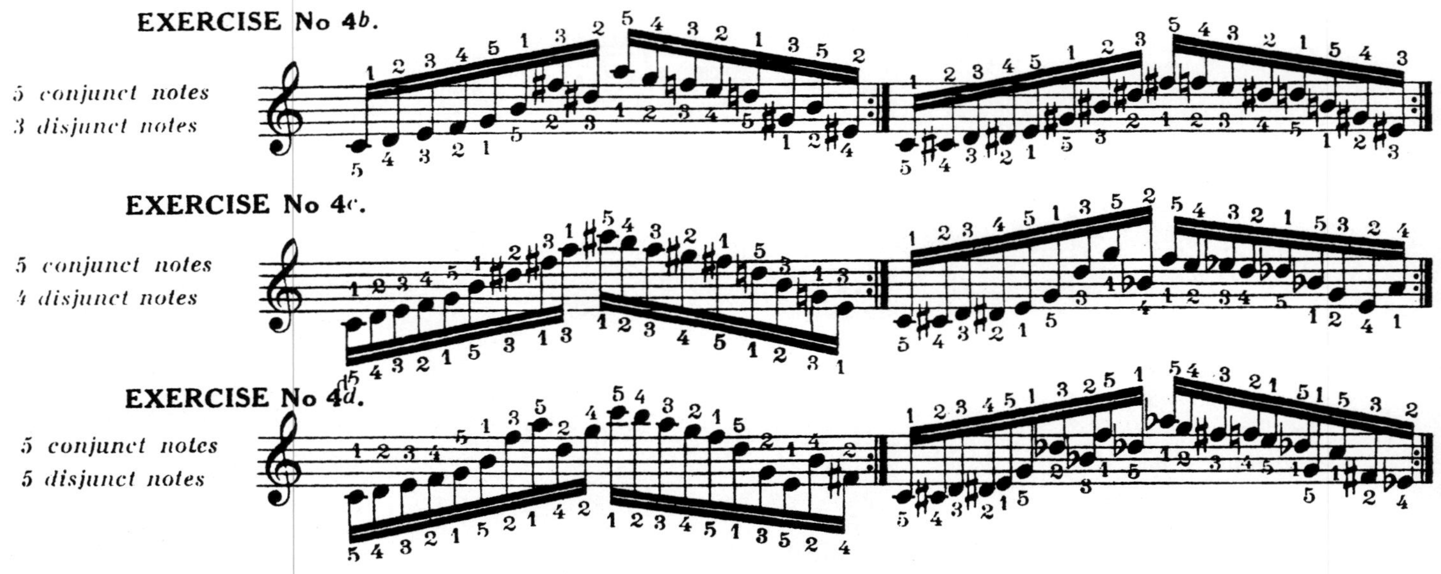

Independently of the variants brought about by the use of the transferable table, to which the signs (C) and (R) refer, we advise that the preceding formulae, should be amplified by the changes of fingering obtained by taking every note of these exercises as a starting point for the thumb, postponing the momentarily omitted notes, to the end of each formula, and by linking together the 32 models just proposed, in an uninterrupted series. The compulsory principle of transposition must naturally not be overlooked.

Complementary Formulae for Exercises

Composed by the Pupil or Recommended by the Teacher

CHAPTER III

The Technique of Double Notes and Polyphonic Playing

Two elements of pianistic technique will be found in this chapter which, although they correspond to musical tendencies of a distinctly different order, are related by a common physiological principle.

The object of one of these, polyphonic playing, is — at any rate considered from the instrumental point of view (which alone occupies our attention here) — the execution, by one hand, of two or more melodic parts, each moving according to its own rhythm and particular design.

This generally proceeds from fugato writing or imitation, and readily submits to the rules of counterpoint. We shall come across it, as the basis of interpretation, in the great works of Bach, Beethoven and Schumann, not to speak of the composers of our times. such as Brahms, Frank or Fauré.

The other, the playing of double notes, is characterised, on the contrary, by the similarity of rhythm of the two parts, which contribute to its formation, its execution likewise being allotted to a single hand.

In most cases the upper part outlines the melodic curve faithfully embraced by the lower voice which follows it note for note, either in parallel, or contrary motion.

The principle of the playing of double notes, is peculiar to ornemental virtuosity, and rests on a tradition of purely harmonic writing. It is particularly manifest in the works of Liszt, Chopin, and the composers who, after them, have turned this brilliant artifice of romantic technique to account.

There is thus no need to be misled by the apparent similarity of the material means brought into play in the two cases. In polyphonic playing it is a question of bringing the various superimposed melodies into prominence, each with its special timbre or rhythm.

In the playing of double notes on the contrary, evenness in volume of tone and equal intensity of the two parts are the rule. The slight predominance in tone generally given to the upper part should only be considered as an instrumental process intended to create a sense of clearness and precision.

The study of double notes should be considered as the best technical preparation for the practice of polyphonic playing.

We therefore insist on the necessity of following the plan of work in this chapter to the letter, and of approaching the exercises in the given order.

The numerous and delicate problems of the execution of part-writing, can only be effectively faced, when the fingers have been previously made supple by the various combinations of Series A and B.

We have confined the formulae for exercises in double notes within the interval of an octave. We consider that when it becomes difficult to finger a succession of intervals, in view of the legato of both parts, it is the technique of the wrist which must intervene. We therefore reserve the study of octaves and wider intervals for Chapter V.

In Chapter IV we propose to facilitate the execution of these intervals, taken separately, by a special preparation in the study of extensions.

SERIES A

The technique of double notes in parallel motion
(Scales and Arpeggios)

The passing under of the thumb, and the sliding of a single finger from one key to the next, having been studied in a preceding chapter, the only preparatory work which remains to be accomplished in order to solve the problem of the execution of double notes in principle, consists in making sure of the perfectly simultaneous attack of the fingers executing the various successions of intervals. The exercises hereafter may be amplified by the student, but it is of the greatest importance that he should submit patiently to their study under the exact form whose elements we provide. He must not be discouraged by the monotonous and lengthy repetition of one and the same example.

EXERCISE No 1a. *(Precision of simultaneous attack : seconds.)*

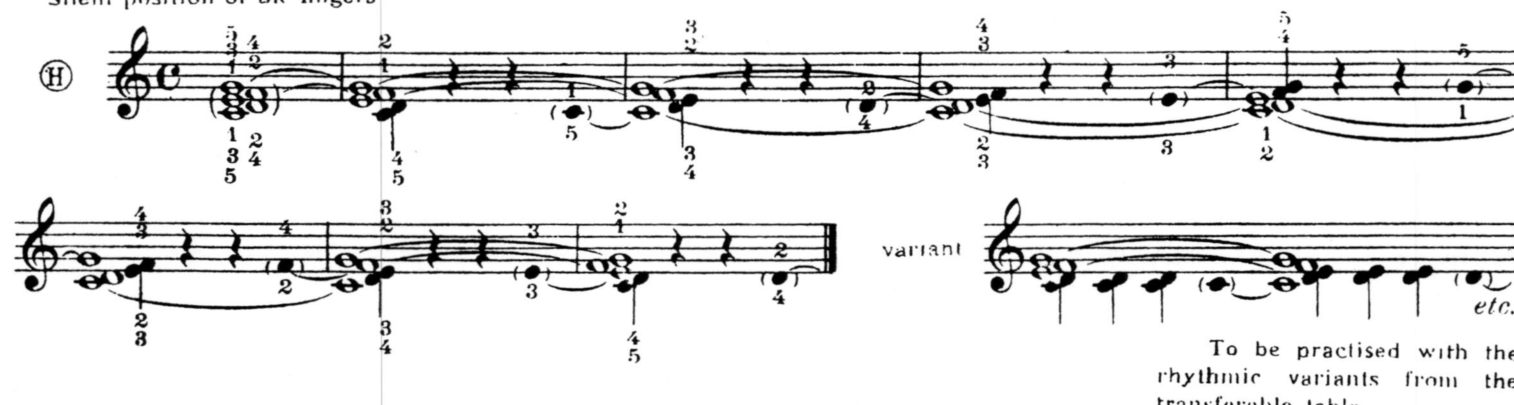

This exercise, as also those which follow, is to be practised thus : Place the fingers on the keys without pressing them down—then play each interval in succession, taking care not to alter the position of the silent fingers. On the fourth beat of each bar let the finger or fingers brought into action on the first beat, regain contact with their keys. These fingers will once more become silent at the next bar, the finger or fingers which continue in action, remaining suspended above their keys and in readiness to strike them.

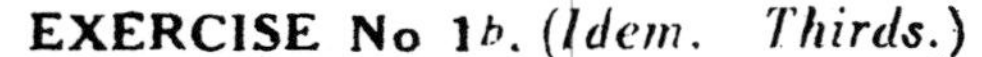

EXERCISE No 1b. *(Idem. Thirds.)*

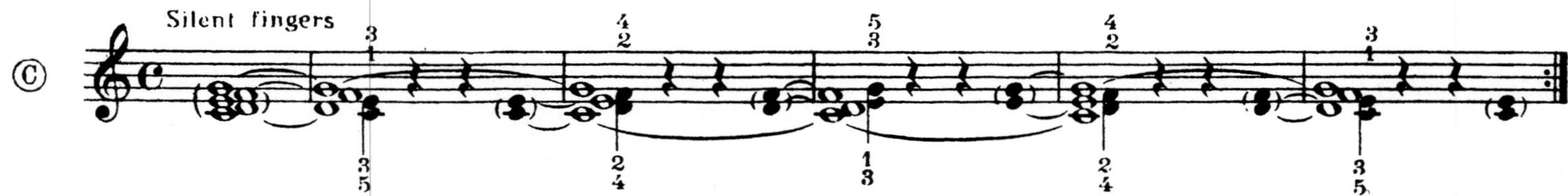

EXERCISE No 1d. *(Idem. Fourths.)*

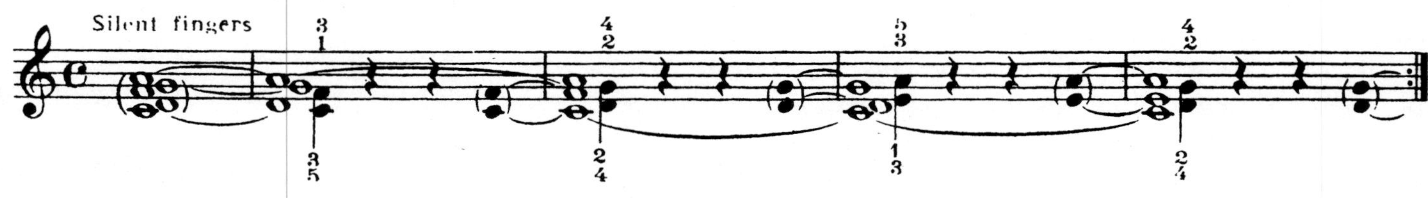

EXERCISE No 1a *(Idem. Fifths.)*

EXERCISE No 1e. *(Idem. Sixths.)*

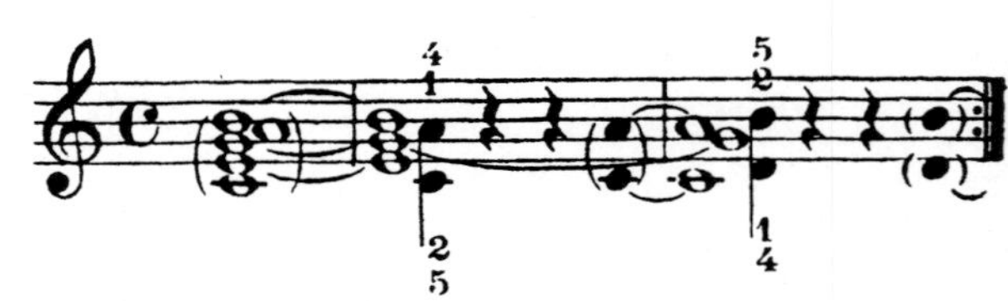

EXERCISE No 1f. *(Idem. Sevenths.)*

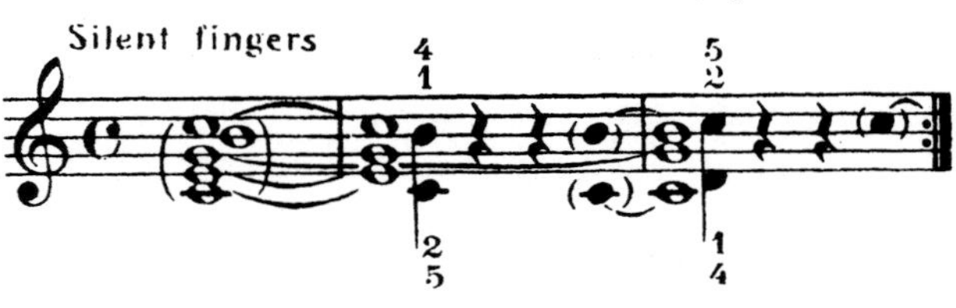

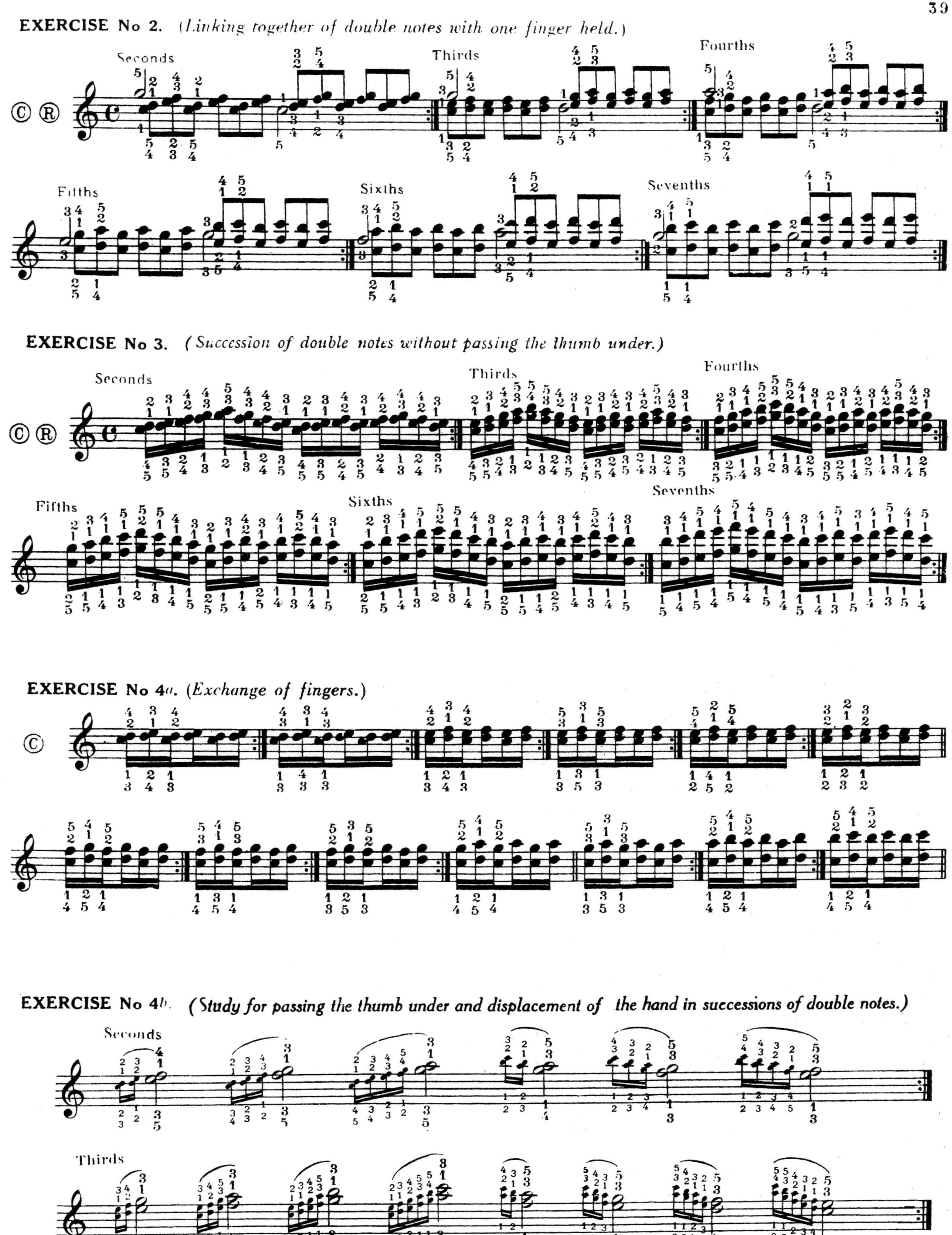
EXERCISE No 2. (Linking together of double notes with one finger held.)
Seconds
Thirds
Fourths
Fifths
Sixths
Sevenths
EXERCISE No 3. (Succession of double notes without passing the thumb under.)
Seconds
Thirds
Fourths
Fifths
Sixths
Sevenths
EXERCISE No 4a. (Exchange of fingers.)
EXERCISE No 4b. (Study for passing the thumb under and displacement of the hand in successions of double notes.)
Seconds
Thirds

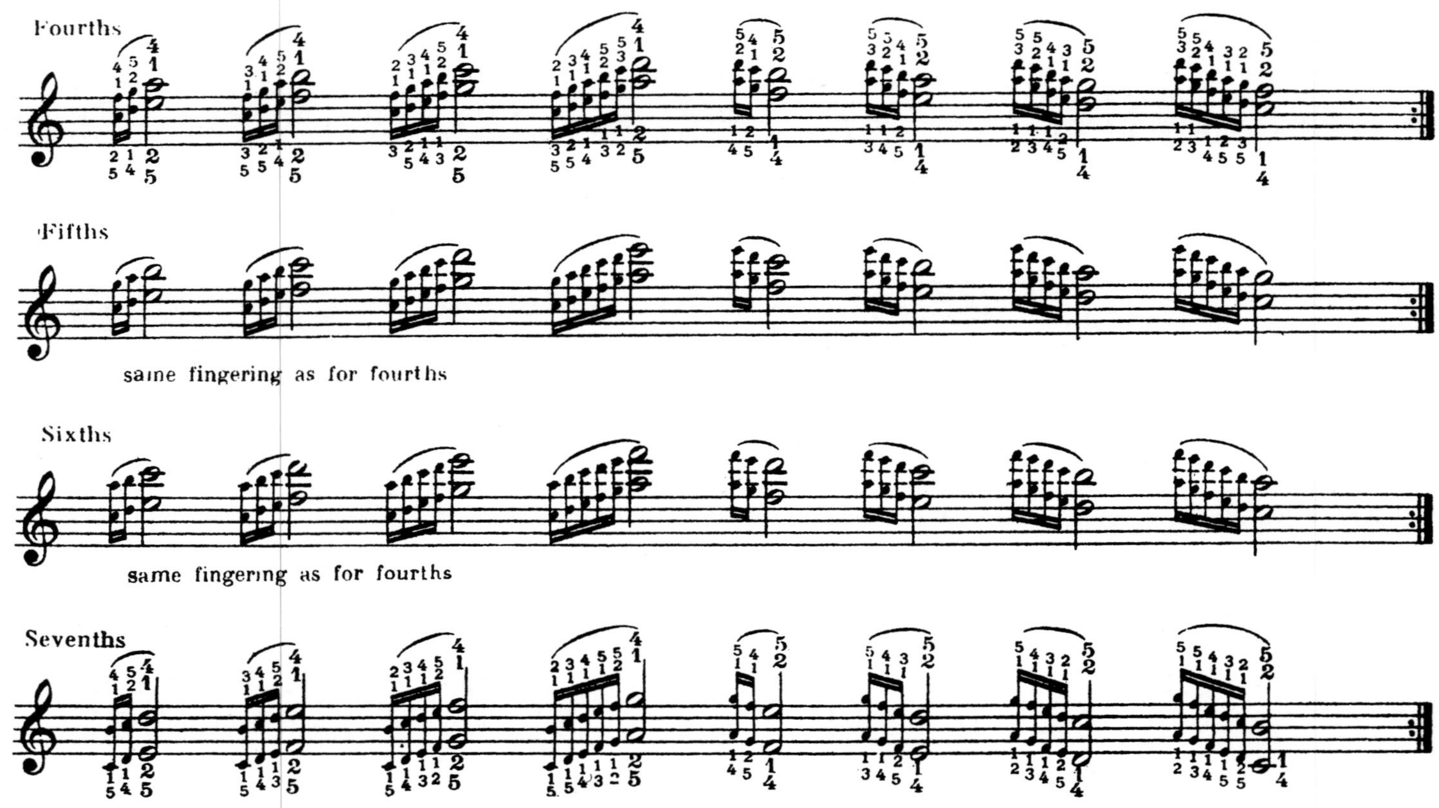

The study of the successions of more than 4 intervals in sixths and all the successions in sevenths should be avoided for small hands. For the different ways of practising this exercise refer to Exercise 4a, Series B, Chapter II.

Diatonic Scales. We approach the study of diatonic scales in double notes, taking into account their frequent use in pianistic works.

The order adopted will therefore be the following: thirds, sixths, fourths, which are in constant use, then fifths, sevenths and seconds, hitherto rarely employed in succession, for reasons of fitness or harmonic tradition, before which, however, the composers of to-day seem less inclined to bow than their predecessors.

We give not only the usual fingering or fingerings of the scales, but also the variations which may be employed according to the exigencies of musical execution. The scales in thirds have the formidable privilege of the most numerous combinations. They all deserve to be studied with the greatest care, as their application to the needs of interpretation constantly imposes itself. It is not therefore a " school for scales " which we intend to lay down here, but a study of all the fingerings required for their execution.

First preliminary exercise for the relation of the fingers to one another in the execution of thirds in conjunction.

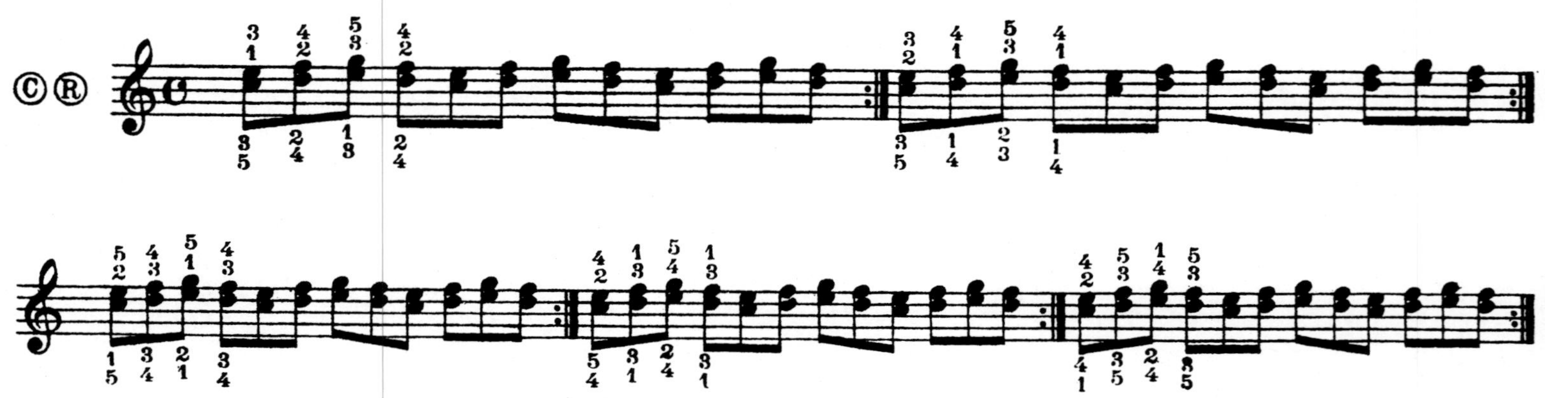

It will already have been observed, during the study of the preceding exercises, that the execution of successions in thirds often entails, for the linking together of two consecutive intervals, the rapid displacement of the third finger which passes from the lower note of the first interval, to the upper note of the second.

This fingering which only permits of a very unsatisfactory legato in both voices, is unfortunately inevitable in many cases.

It will be the object of a special exercise below :

2nd preliminary exercise, transmission of the third finger.

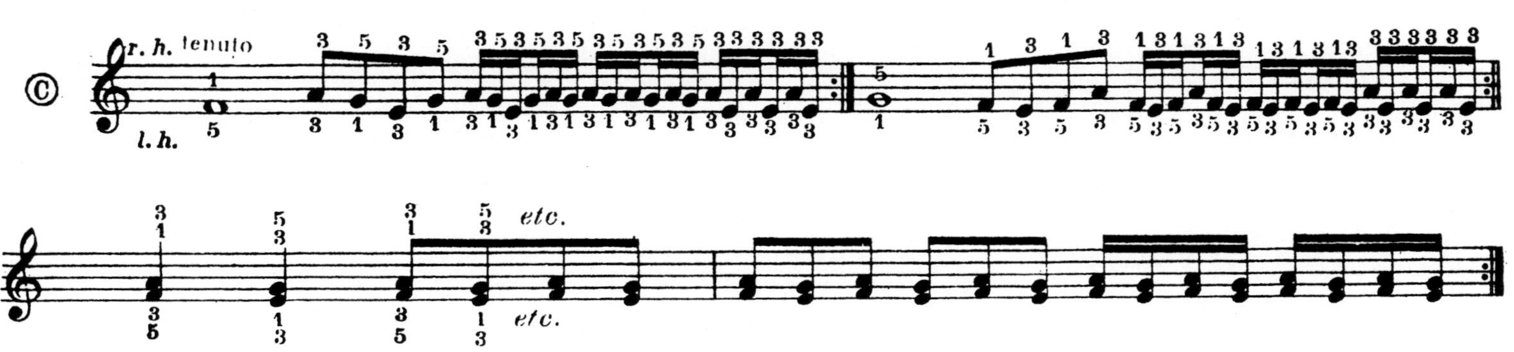

EXERCISE No 5*a*. (*Scales in thirds.*)

Apply these fingerings to the following types of scales.

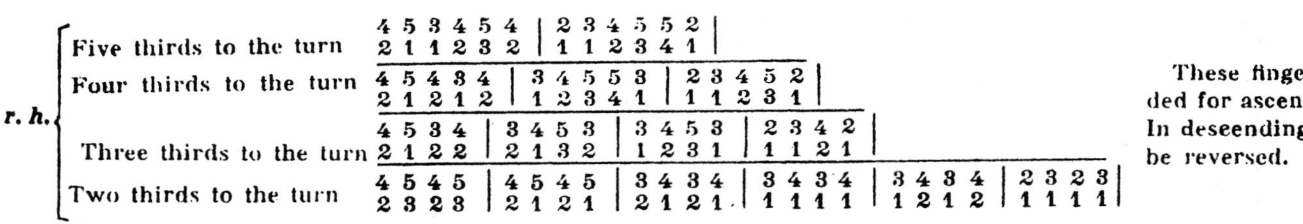

r. h.						
Five thirds to the turn	4 5 3 4 5 4 2 1 1 2 3 2	2 3 4 5 5 2 1 1 2 3 4 1				
Four thirds to the turn	4 5 4 3 4 2 1 2 1 2	3 4 5 5 3 1 2 3 4 1	2 3 4 5 2 1 1 2 3 1			
Three thirds to the turn	4 5 3 4 2 1 2 2	3 4 5 3 2 1 3 2	3 4 5 3 1 2 3 1	2 3 4 2 1 1 2 1		
Two thirds to the turn	4 5 4 5 2 3 2 3	4 5 4 5 2 1 2 1	3 4 3 4 2 1 2 1	3 4 3 4 1 1 1 1	3 4 3 4 1 2 1 2	2 3 2 3 1 1 1 1

These fingerings are provided for ascending succession. In deseending they need only be reversed.

l. h.						
Five thirds to the turn	4 3 2 1 1 4 5 5 4 3 2 5	2 1 1 2 1 2 4 5 3 4 3 4				
Four thirds to the turn	3 2 1 1 3 5 4 3 2 5	4 3 2 1 4 5 5 4 3 5	2 1 2 1 2 4 5 4 3 4			
Three thirds to the turn	2 1 1 2 4 3 2 4	3 2 1 3 5 4 3 5	3 1 2 3 5 4 3 5	2 1 2 2 3 5 4 3		
Two thirds to the turn	1 1 1 1 3 2 3 2	2 1 2 1 4 3 4 3	1 1 1 1 4 3 4 3	1 2 1 2 4 3 4 3	1 2 1 2 5 4 5 4	3 2 3 2 5 4 5 4

EXERCISE No 5*b*. *(Mixed fingerings, same type of scale.)*

Combinations

		Combination	Fingering	
r. h.	1)	3 fingers 4	5 4 5 2 3 4 5 / = 1 2 3 1 1 2 3	etc.
	2)	4 " + 3	2 3 4 5 3 4 5 / = 1 1 2 3 1 2 3	etc.
	3)	5 " + 5 + 3	3 4 3 4 3 4 5 / = 1 2 1 2 1 2 3	etc.
	4)	3 " + 5 + 5	3 4 5 3 4 3 4 / = 1 2 3 1 2 1 2	etc.
	5)	5 " + 3 + 5	3 4 3 4 5 3 4 / = 1 2 1 2 3 1 2	etc.
l. h.	1)	3 " + 4	3 2 1 3 2 1 1 / = 5 4 3 5 4 3 2	etc.
	2)	4 " + 3	3 2 1 1 3 2 1 / = 5 4 3 2 5 4 3	etc.
	3)	5 " + 5 + 3	2 1 2 1 3 2 1 / = 4 3 4 3 5 4 3	etc.
	4)	3 " + 5 + 5	3 2 1 2 1 2 1 / = 5 4 3 4 3 4 3	etc.
	5)	5 " + 3 + 5	2 1 3 2 1 2 1 / = 4 3 5 4 3 4 3	etc.

Finger inversely in descending.
The fingerings of Nos. 1 and 2 are the usual fingerings of the scale.

EXERCISE No 5*c*. *(Regular fingering for several octaves.)*

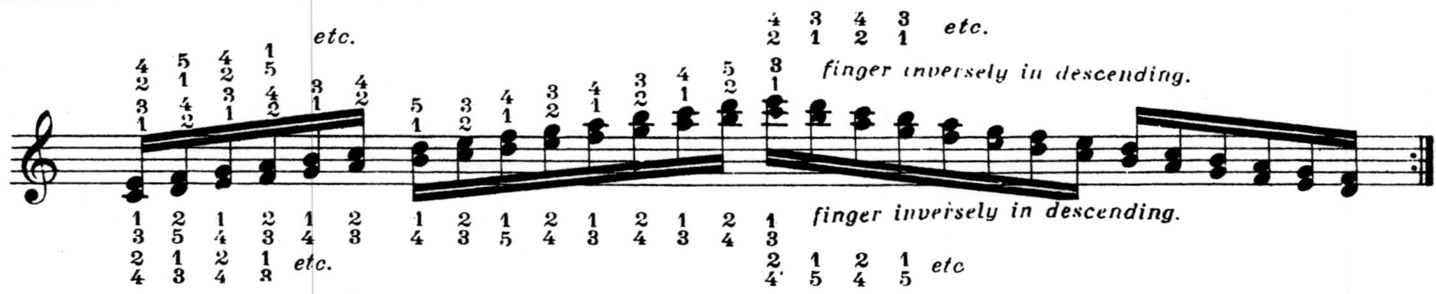

These two last fingerings are used for choice in the key of C major, but we recommend their study in all keys.

EXERCISE No 6 *(Scales in Sixths)*

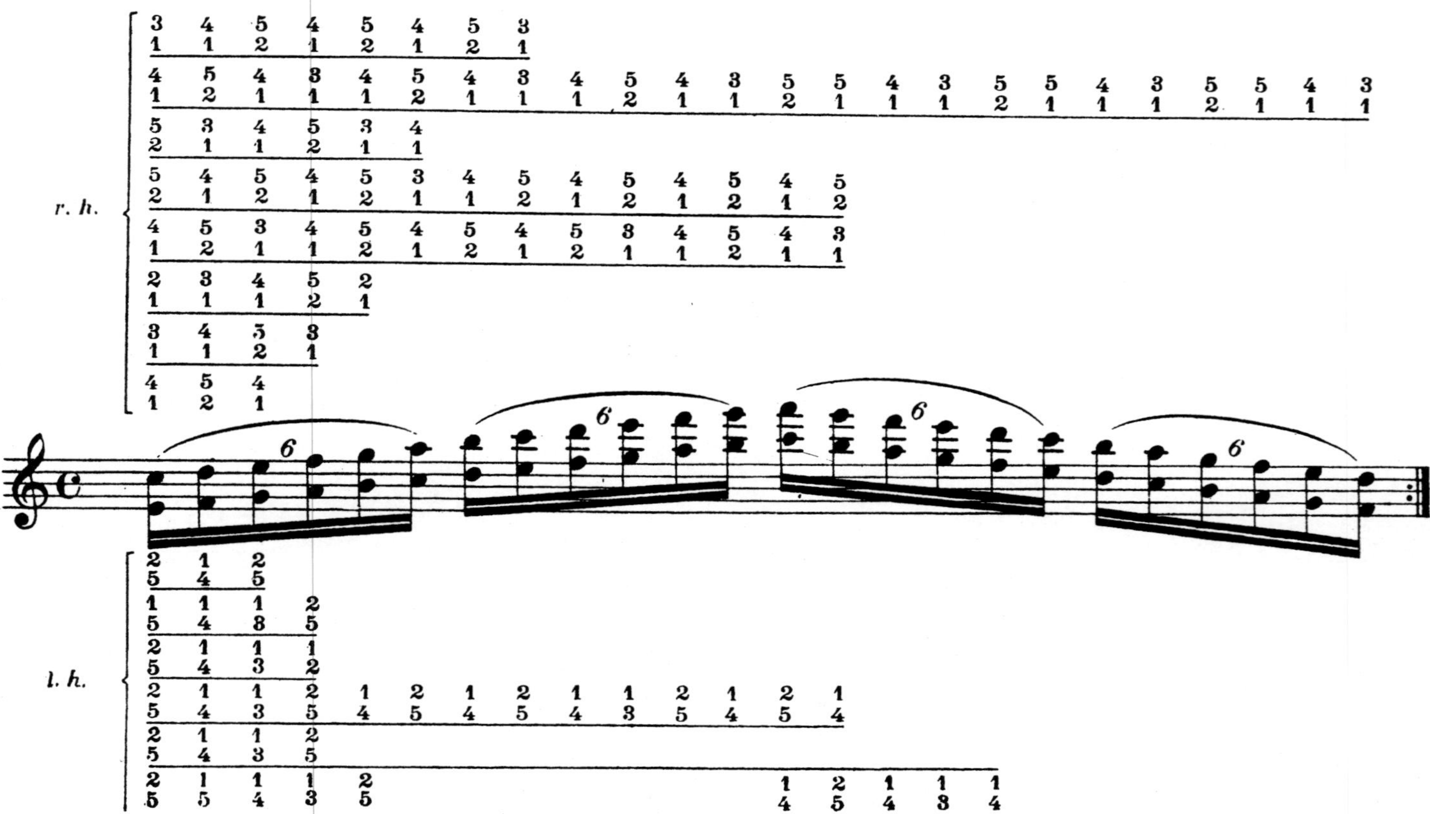

EXERCISE No 7. *(Scales in fourths)*

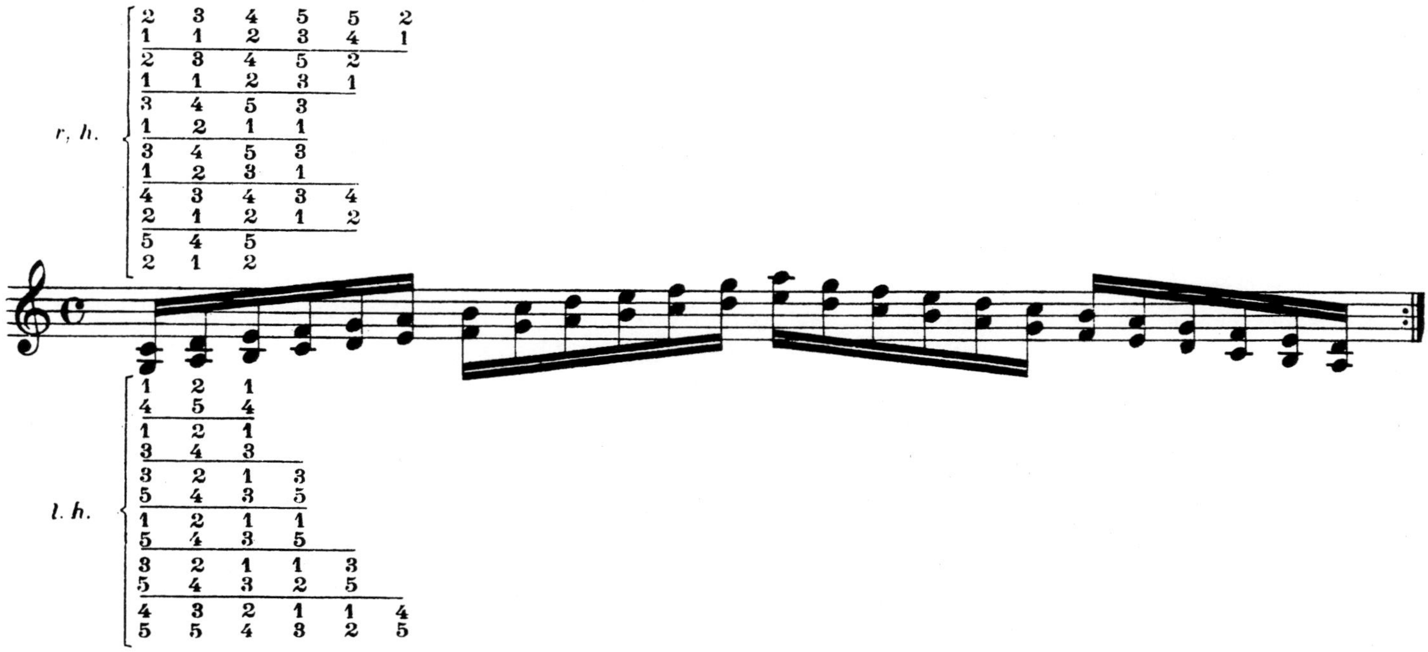

We mention that, apart from the above fingerings, all the combinations precedingly indicated for thirds (Ex. N° 5 and its variations) are equally applicable to scales in fourths, with the exception of certain formulae which would cause an exaggerated extension for short fingered hands. The teacher must decide on the choice to be made.

EXERCISE No 8 *(Scales in fifths)*

EXERCISE No 9 *(Scales in sevenths)*

* The fingering marked by this sign is to be practised by long fingered hands only.

EXERCISE No 10 (*Scales in seconds*)

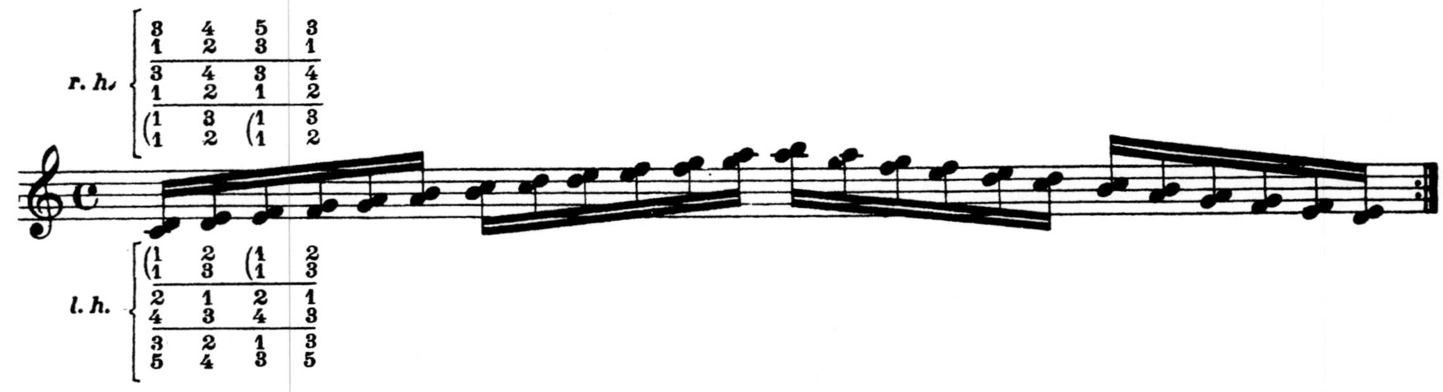

It will be noticed, in the first fingering given for the succession of seconds, that the thumb strikes two notes each time it plays. This fingering is certainly the smoothest of the three we mentioned, but it can only be utilised in the C major key. All these types of scales are also to be practised in broken form, with the fingerings precedingly indicated.

This is especially advised for short fingered hands.

Double notes in disjunct motion (arpeggios) and broken chords,

EXERCISE No 2.

A. *On intervals of the second.*

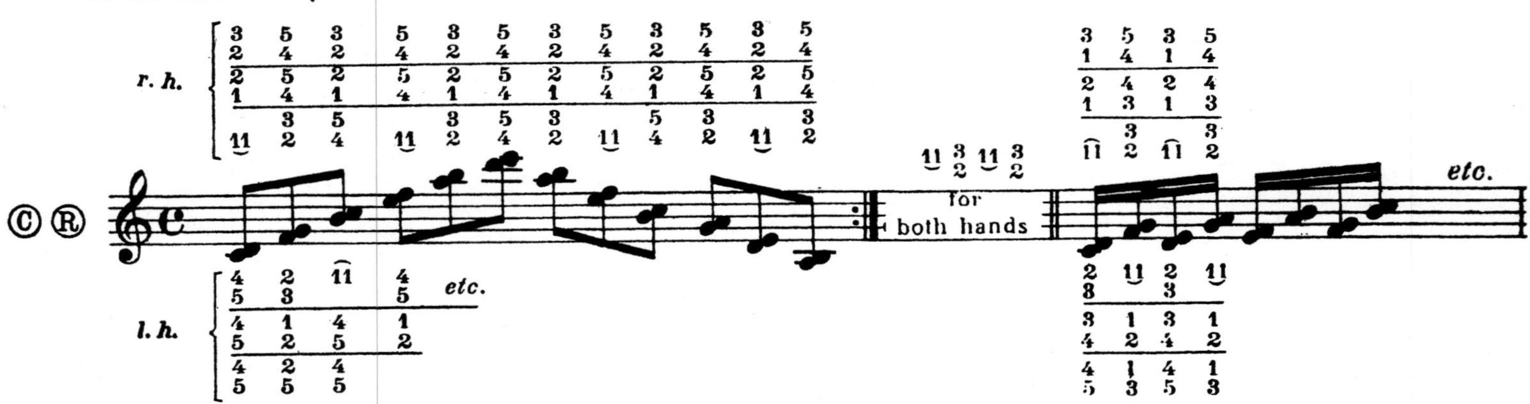

B. *On intervals of the third.*

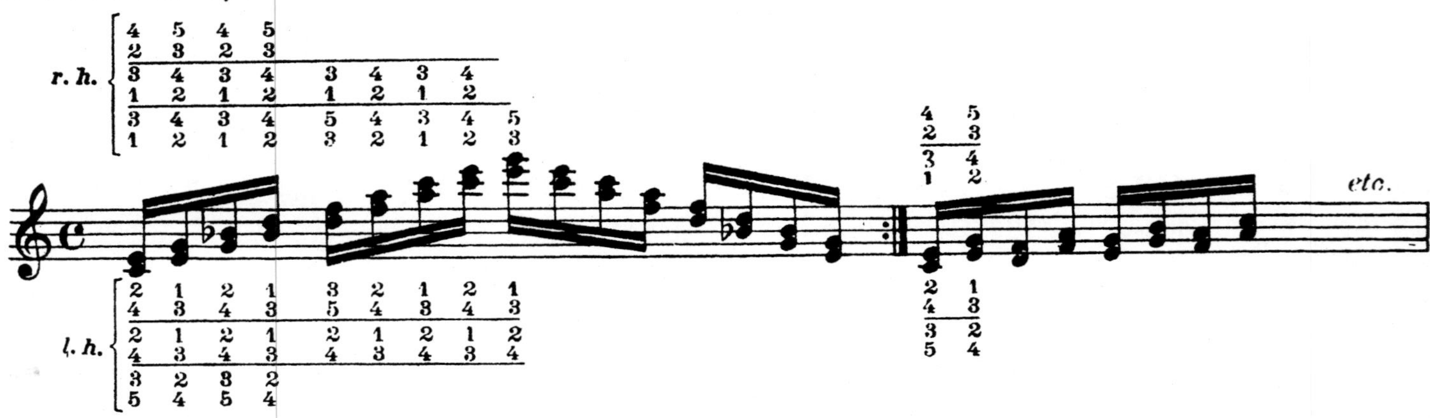

C. *On intervals of the fourth.*

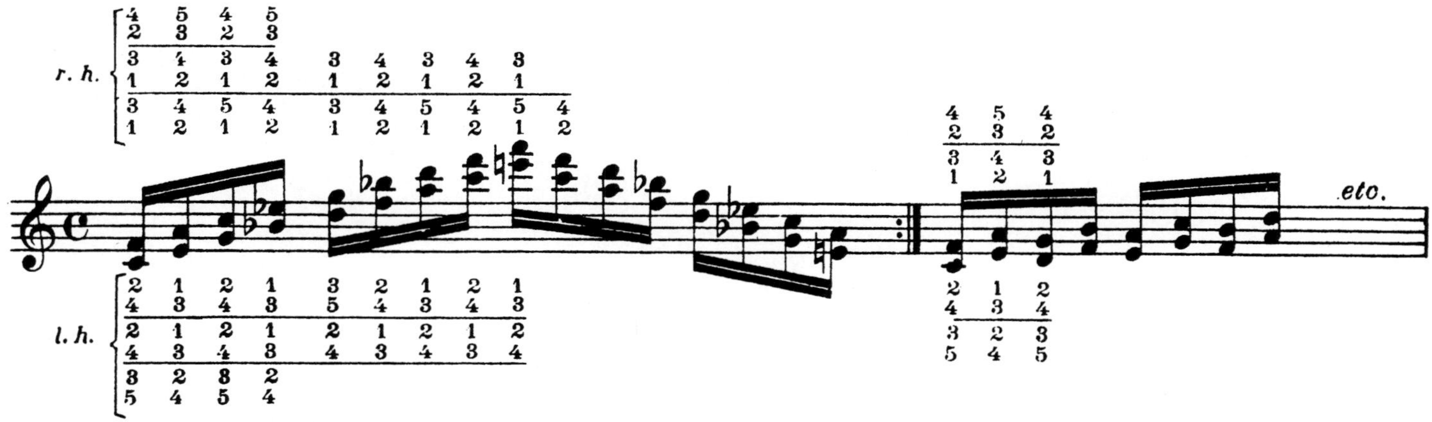

D. *On intervals of the fifth.*

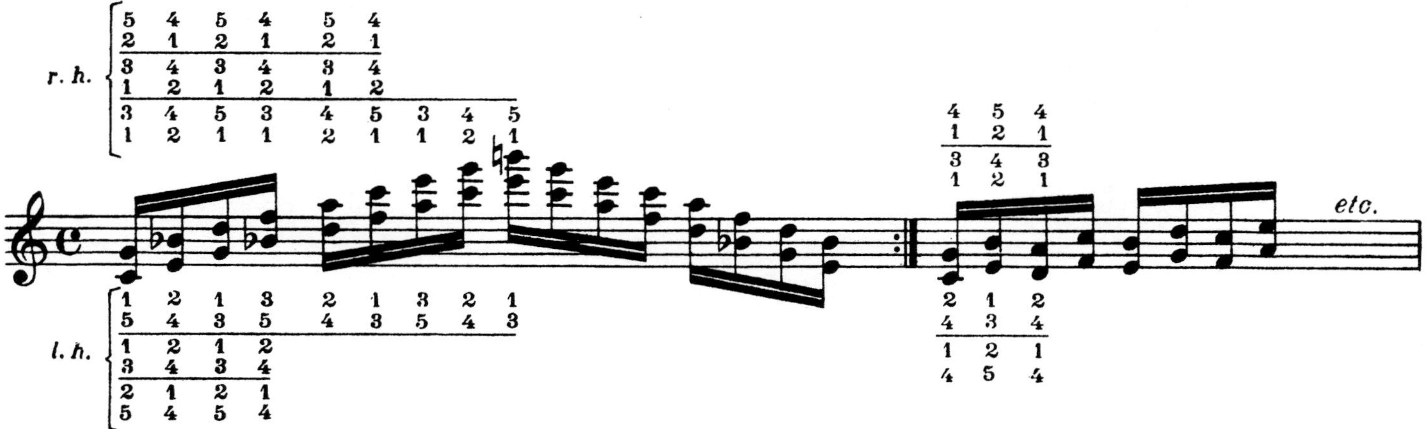

E. *On intervals of the sixth.*

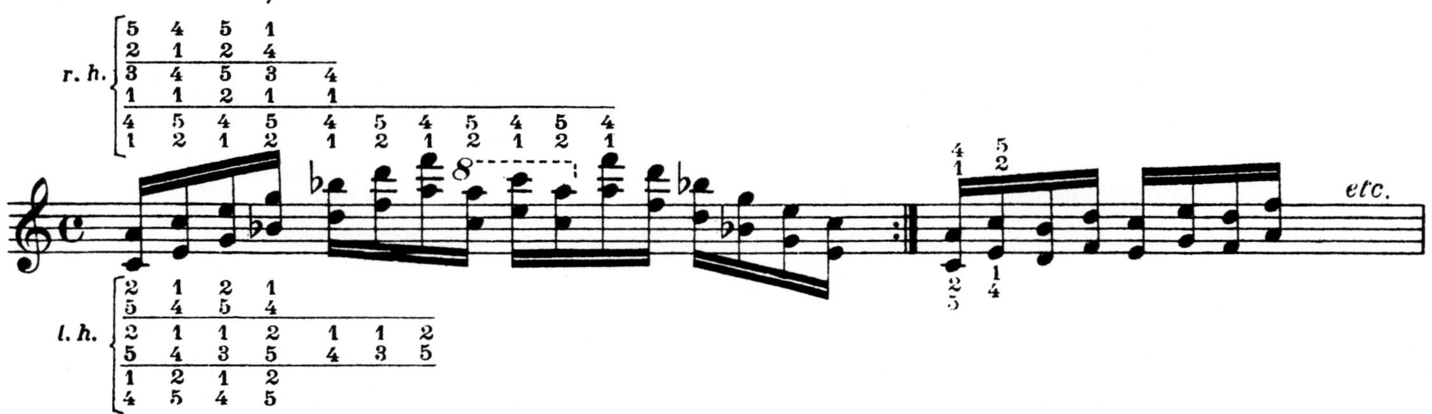

F. *On intervals of the seventh.*

We recommend for this exercise, as well as for the next, a preliminary study based on the model of exercise No. 4 **Series A** of the same Chapter.

EXERCISE No 3*a*. *(Mixed intervals on forms of the arpeggio in double notes, in parallel motion.)*

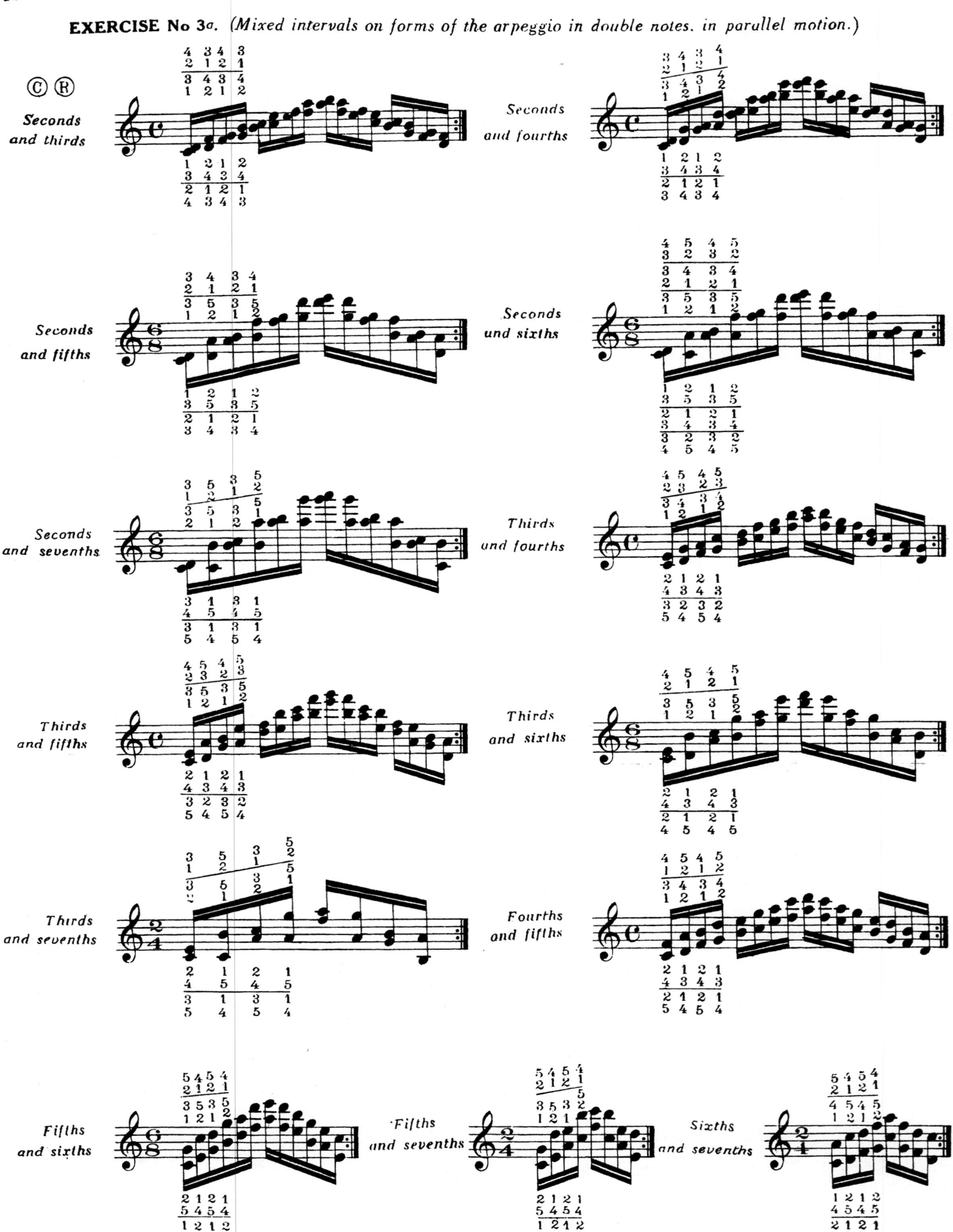

EXERCISE No 3b. (*Succession of various intervals in parallel motion, summing up the whole of the combinations of fingering.*)

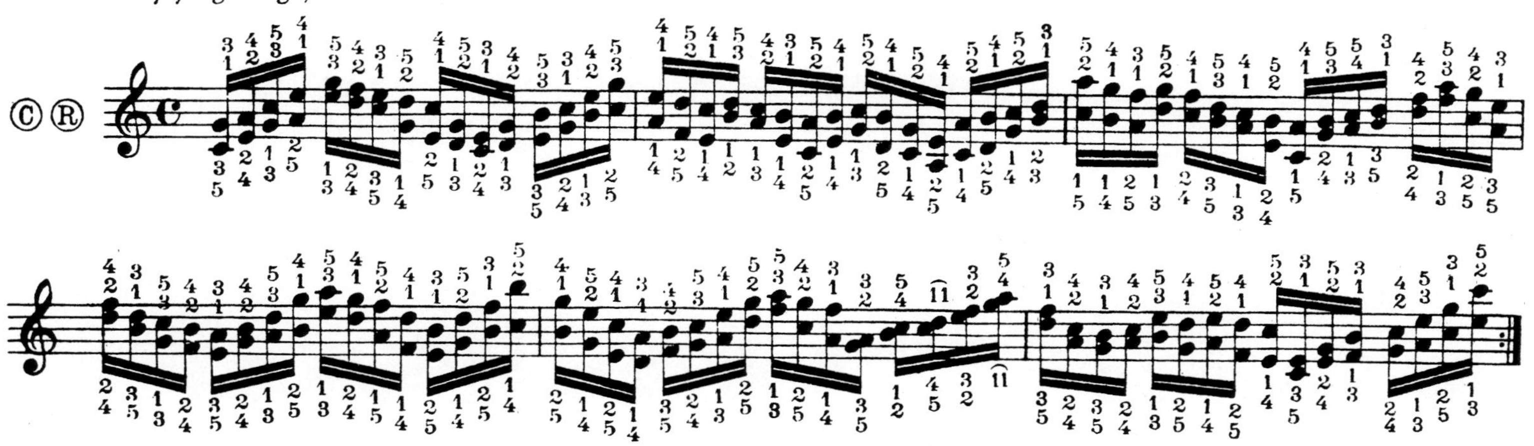

For these exercises we recommend the following variants :

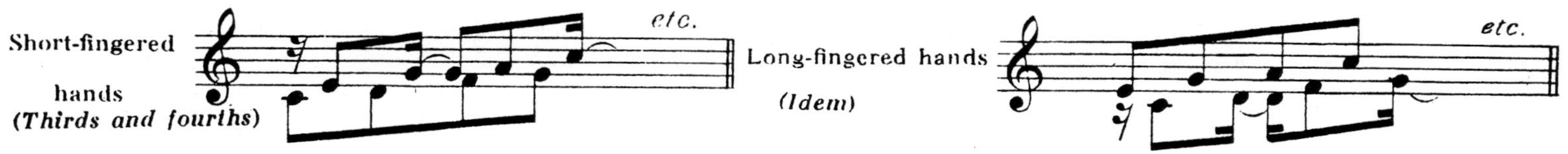

SERIES B

The Technique of double notes in parallel motion (continued)

Chromatic Successions. — In a chromatic scale in double notes, the interval employed remains uniform throughout the scale. In diatonic scales, owing to the laws of modality, chords of the same kind become major or minor according to the degrees on which they occur. This entails the use of a slightly different technique in each of these cases.

The difficulties offered by the execution of chromatic double notes, are, on the whole, not so great as the difficulties of diatonic progressions. The uniformity of their intervals, just described, their constant use of keys in the closest proximity for the successions of the fingers, abolish many of the complications encountered above.

But the frequent sliding of one finger, other than the thumb, from a black key to the adjacent white one. the crossing of the upper fingers of the right hand. or the lower ones of the left. the use, in spite of the succession of notes being the same, of a different fingering in one of the voices, according to whether the interval is major or minor, augmented, perfect or diminished, will require very special attention and will direct our work along a clearly defined path.

We make a study of these technical peculiarities in the following exercises. A table of three fingerings will be found for each model of the scale — two for study, and one for execution. The first provides for the repetition, at regular intervals, of a rigorously identical combination of fingers. This systematic principle, not generally suitable to musical execution, will however infallibly insure gymnastic independence of the fingers and suppleness in the displacements of the hand.

The second is more especially concerned with the sliding of one finger from one note to another. on two or more keys. and with the crossing of various fingers. Finally the third offers, not only the most usual fingerings, but also the majority of those which pianistic ingenuity has, in later years. placed at the disposal of the virtuoso.

These cannot be overlooked in the elaboraion of a complete technique.

EXERCISE No 1. *(Chromatic scales in double notes on all intervals.)*

The transposition of the chromatic scale naturally does not come into question the degrees of which it is constituted being identical in all keys.

A. *Minor seconds.*

B. *Major seconds*

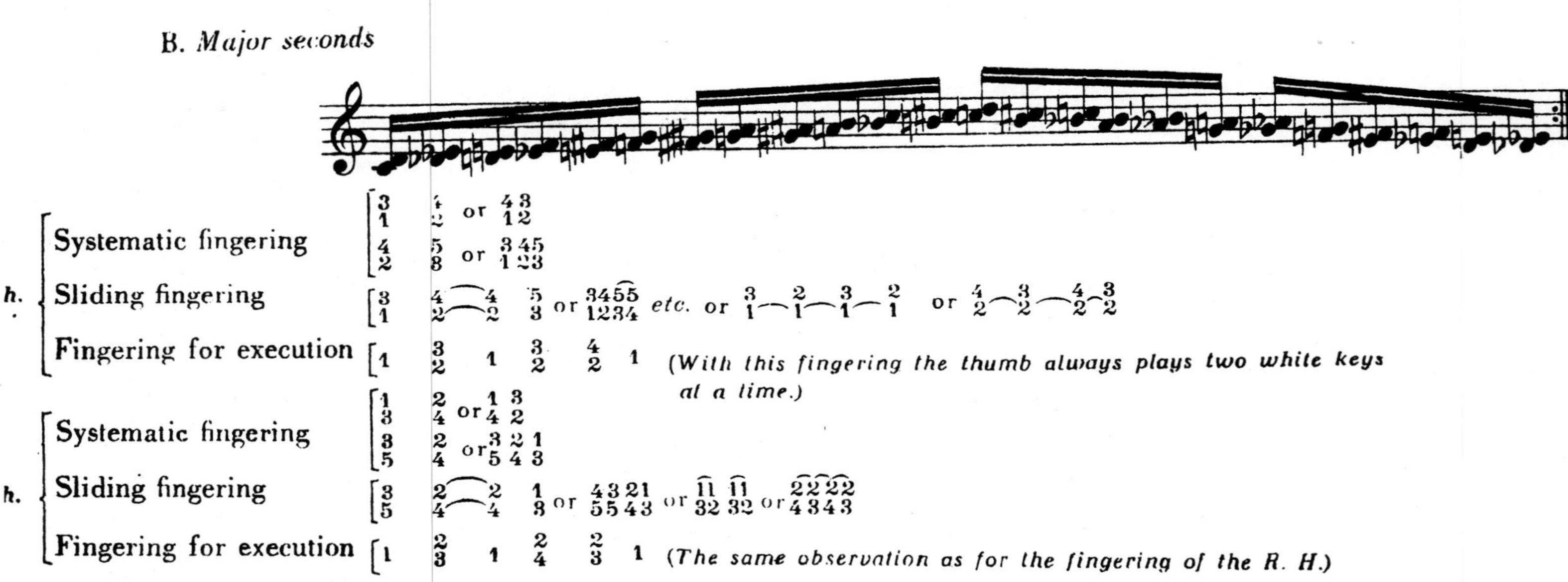

C. *Minor thirds.* (Enharmonically augmented seconds.)

r. h.

Systematic fingering

3 4 or 34 or 4 5 or 45 or 4 5 or 54
1 2 or 21 or 1 2 or 21 or 2 3 or 32

3 4 5
1 2 3

Sliding fingering

2 3 or 34 or 35 or 45 or 45 or 3455 or 23 4 55 or (44 5 3433 44 5 33)
1⌒1 or 11 or 11 or 11 or 22 or 1234 or 11 2 34 or (12 1 2212 12 1 22)

Fingering for execution

3 4 5 3 4 3 4 3 4 5 3 4 3 5 4 3 4 3 4 3 5 4 3 4
1 2 1 2 1⌒1 2 1 2 1 2 1⌒1 3 2 1 2 1 2 1 3 2 1 2

3 4 5 4 5 3 4 5 3
1 2 1 2⌒2 1 2⌒2 1

3 4 3 4
2⌒2 2⌒2

3 4 3 4 3 4 5 3 4 3 4 5 3
1 2 1 2 1 2 3 1 2 1 2 3 1

4 5 4 3 5 4 5 4 3 5 4
2 3 1 2 1 1 2 1 2 1 2

3 4 5 4 5 4 5 3 4 5 4 5 4
1 2 1 2 1 3 2 1 2 1 2 1 3

3 4 5 4 3 4 5
2⌒2 1 2 2⌒2 1

4 4 5 4 5 4
2 2 3 2 1 2

1 4 5 3 4 3 3
3 2 3 1 2 1 1

5 4 5 5
1 2 1 1

3 4 3 4 3 4 5 3 4 3 4
2 1 1 2 1 2 1 2 1 1 2

4 3 3 3 4
2 1 1 2 1

l. h.

Systematic fingering

2 1 or 12 or 2 1 or 12 or 3 2 or 23
4 3 or 43 or 5 4 or 54 or 5 4 or 45

3 2 1
5 4 3

Sliding fingering

1⌒1 or 11 or 11 or 11 or 22 or 43 21 or 43211 or 22 121212 22 121
3 2 or 43 or 53 or 34 or 54 or 5543 or 55432 or 4 3 5444343 543

Fingering for execution

2 1 3 2 1 2 1 2 1 3 2 1 2 1 2 1 1 2 1 2 1 2 1 2 2
4 3 5 4 3 4 3 4 3 5 4 3 4 5 3 4 3 4 3 4 5 3 4 3 4

2 1 2⌒2 2⌒2 1 2
4 5 3 4 3 4 3 4

2⌒2 2⌒2 1 2
4 5 4 5 3 4

2⌒2 1 2 1 2 1 2⌒2 1 2 1 2
4 3 5 4 5 4 3 4 3 5 4 3 4

3 2 1 2 1 3 2 1⌒1 3 2 1
5 4 3 4 3 5 4 3 2 5 4 3

3 2 1 3 2 1⌒1 3 2 1 3 2 1
5 4 3 5 4 3 2 5 4 3 5 4 3

1 2 1 2 1 2 1 2 1⌒1 2 1 2
4 3 4 3 5 4 3 4 3 5 3 5 4

2 1 2 1⌒1 2 1 4 3 5 3 5 1
5 4 5 4 3 5 4 5 4 3 5 4 3

2 1⌒1 2 1 2 1 2 1⌒1 2 1 1
4 3⌒2 4 3 4 3 4 3 2 4 3 2

3 2 3 2 1 3 2 1⌒1 3 2⌒2 1
5 4 5 4 3 5 4 3 2 5 4 5 4

3 1⌒1 2 1 2 1 3 1⌒1 2 1 2
5 4 3 4 3 4 3 5 4 3 4 3 4

D. *Major thirds.* (Enharmonically diminished fourths.)

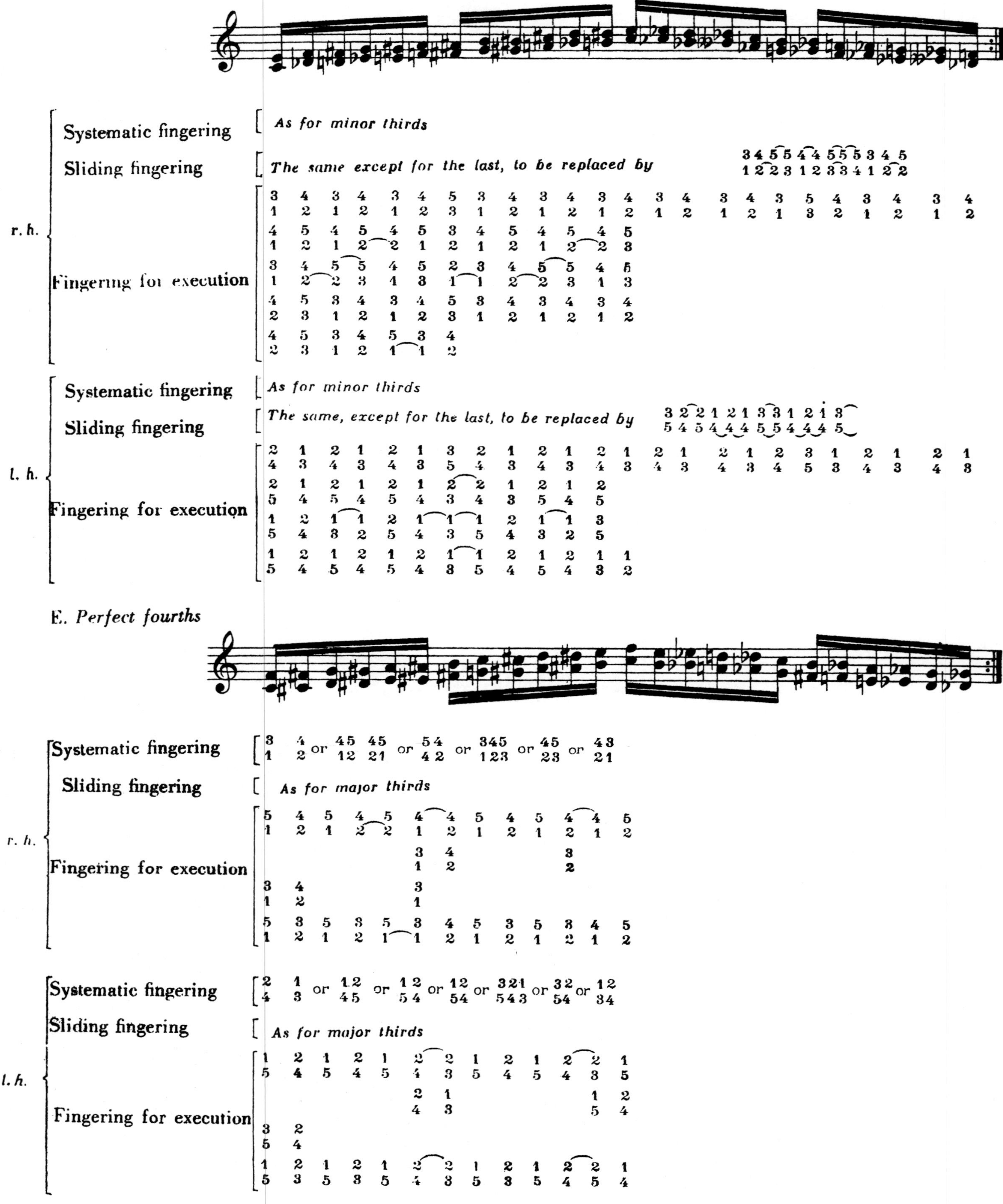

F. *Augmented fourths.* (Enharmonically — diminished fifths.)

r. h.
Systematic fingering — *As for the perfect fourths with the exception, for short-fingered hands, of the two last fingerings.*
Sliding fingering
Fingering for execution

l. h.
Systematic fingering — *See observation above.*
Sliding fingering
Fingering for execution

G. *Perfect fifths.*

r. h.
Systematic fingering
Sliding fingering
Fingering for execution

l. h.
Systematic fingering
Sliding fingering
Fingering for execution

H. *Minor sixths.* (Enharmonically — augmented fifths.)

r. h.
Systematic fingering
Sliding fingering
Fingering for execution

l. h.
Systematic fingering
Sliding fingering
Fingering for execution

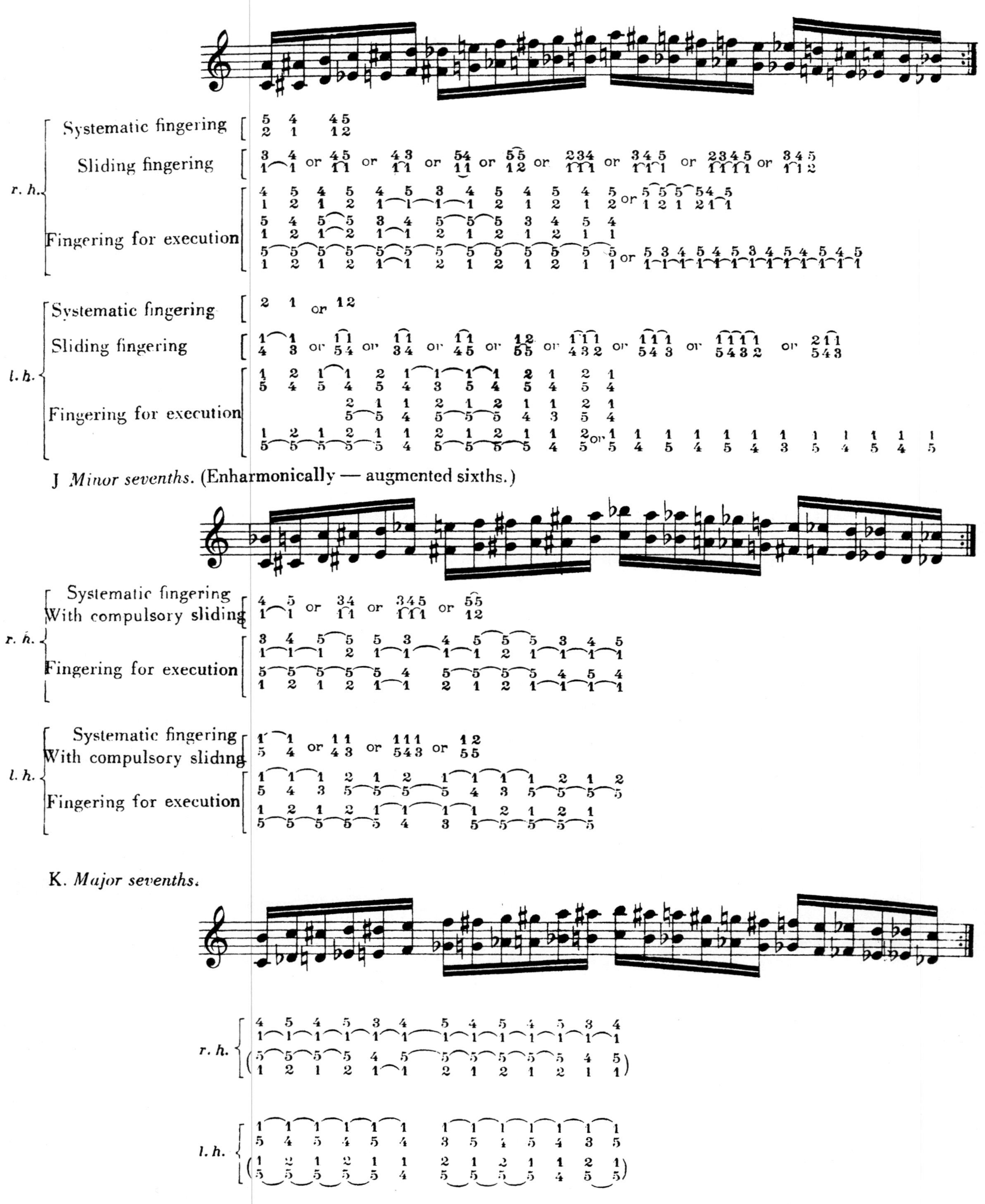

The three fingerings here become one, which is the fingering for execution. The variant in parentheses is only to be studied with great prudence, and by long fingered hands alone.

L. *Octaves (same observation).*

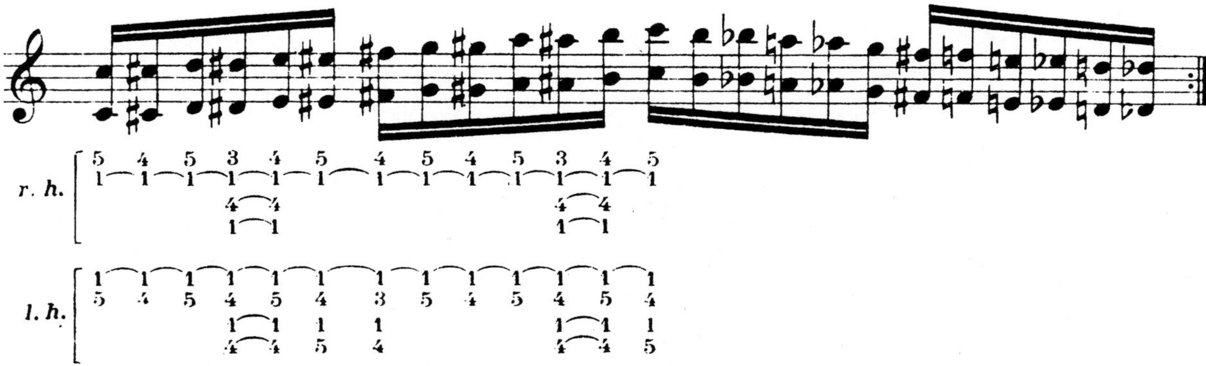

In spite of the reservation made above, concerning the study of this interval in the present chapter, we nevertheless here indicate the fingerings befitting a legato execution of it, when in chromatic succession, as the latter affords a less accentuated participation of the movements of the wrist, than its execution in diatonic form.

SERIES C

Polyphonic technique

At the beginning of this chapter, we laid stress on the importance of polyphonic technique, in the interpretation of the works of Bach and Beethoven.

We ought to generalise more fully, and extend its influence to the majority of the key-board works of the German school, dating from the Reformation.

For a development occurred in Germany at that time, which was the very reverse of that which was happening in Italy or in France, where we see, in the course of the 18th century, the gallant style of the harpsichordists, with their florid and brilliant grace of writing, gradually being introduced into the repertory of the church, and making the organists of the day forget the magnificent expressive discipline of a Titelouze or a Frescobaldi, so powerfully nurtured by the strong resources of plain-song; while at the same period, in Germany, we find on the contrary, a profane music pervaded throughout by the accents of the Protestant choral.

We should be overstepping the bounds which are set us by the purely specialised character of this work, if we attempted an analysis of the various reasons for the superiority of German instrumental music, from this date up to the middle of the nineteenth century.

But we shall have laid sufficient emphasis on the artistic importance of the kind of execution studied in the examples in this series, if we admit that the abandonment of the polyphonic style, by the countries of Catholic tradition, brought about, as a momentary consequence, their renunciation of a musical supremacy which they had held for centuries.

Apart from quality of tone, and researches in individual timbres for each voice — a question whose study finds no place in a work of purely gymnastic pianism — the difficulties inherent in all polyphonic execution, reside in the complexity of the rhythms allotted to the fingers of a single hand, and the divergent movements of these fingers on the key-board.

It is to an analysis of these two technical principles, that we shall limit the part which we may aspire to play in the examination of one of the problems of virtuosity which cannot — as we have just pointed out — be solved by the fingers alone.

But if we may not here attempt to approach the question in its fullest musical sense, we are at least certain that the study of the preparatory excercises which follow, will result in the knowledge of its essential technical characteristics.

EXERCISE No 1a. *(Technique of double notes in contrary motion.)*

These exercises are to be practised separately, sometimes playing the upper part legato and the lower part staccato, and sometimes vice versa; the legato part always *piano* and the staccato part always *forte*.

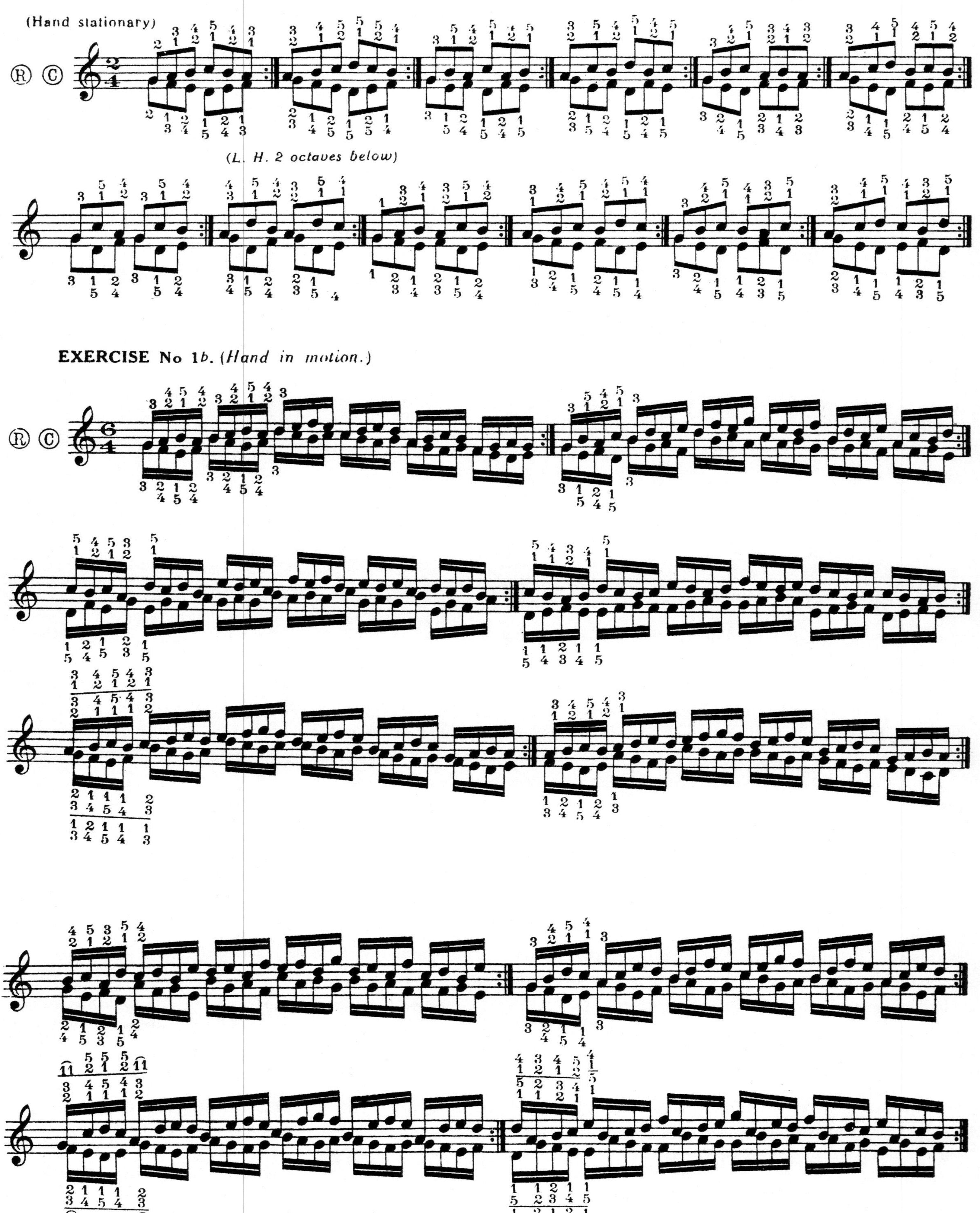

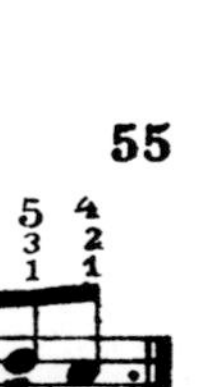

EXERCISE No 2. (*Triple notes.*) Ⓡ Ⓒ

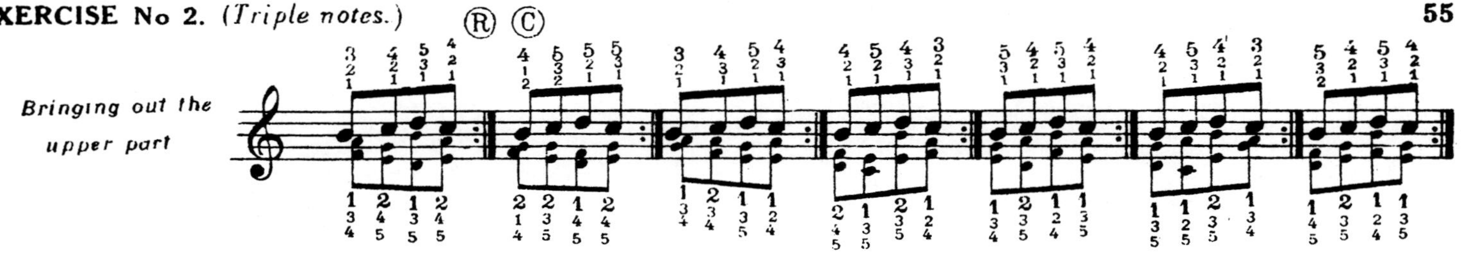

EXERCISE No 3*a*. (*Opposing rhythms in 2 parts—one note against two.*)

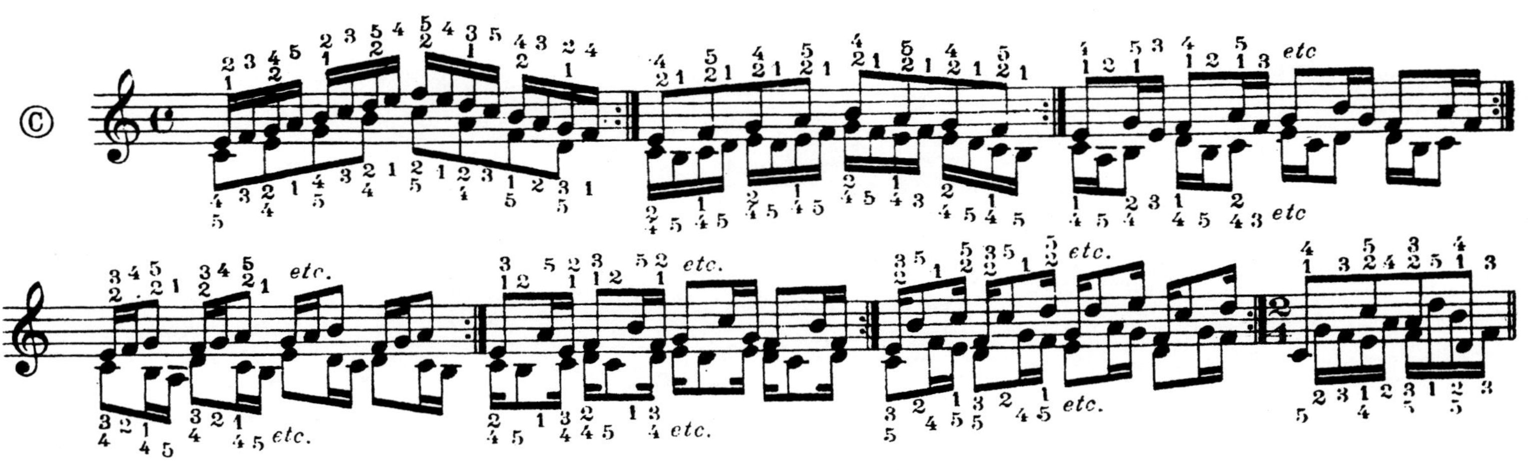

EXERCISE No 3*b*. (*1 note against 3.*)

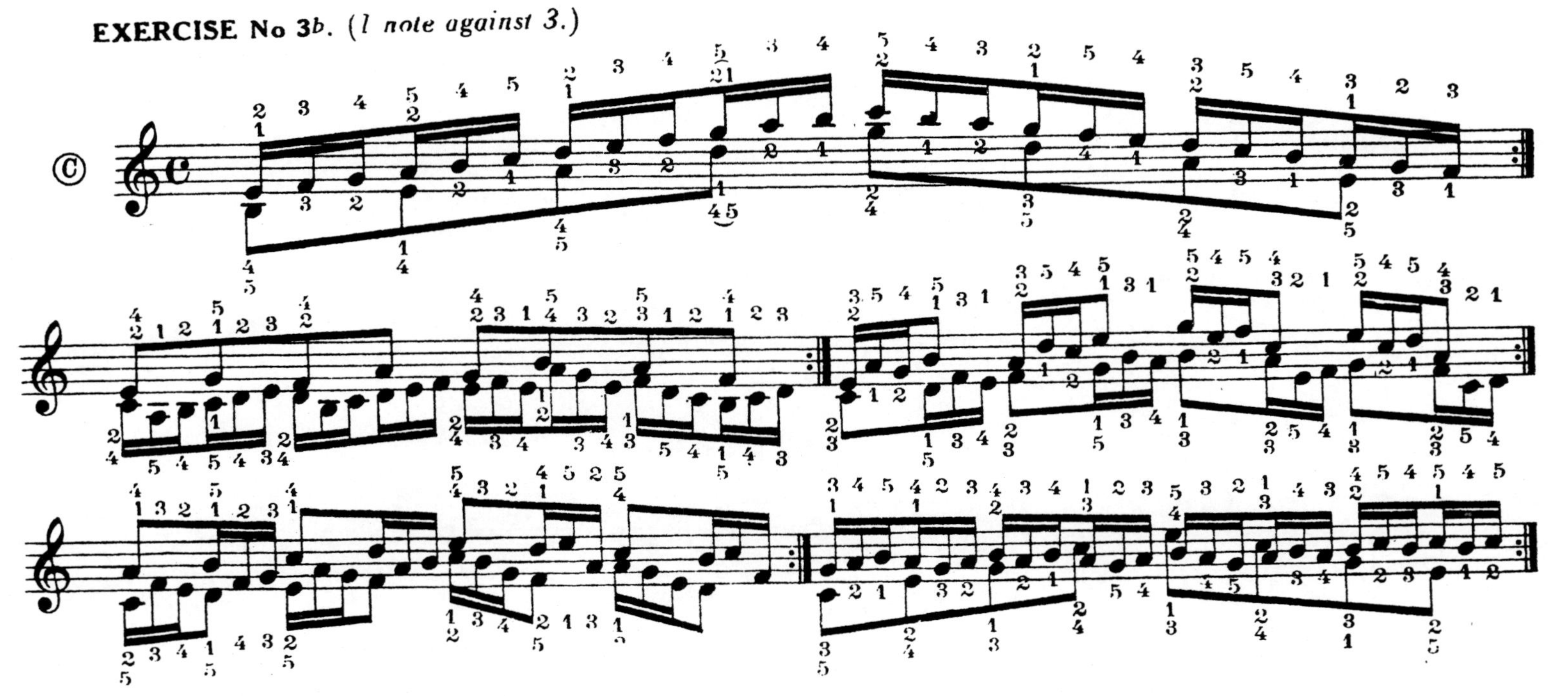

EXERCISE No 3c. *(1 note against 4.)*

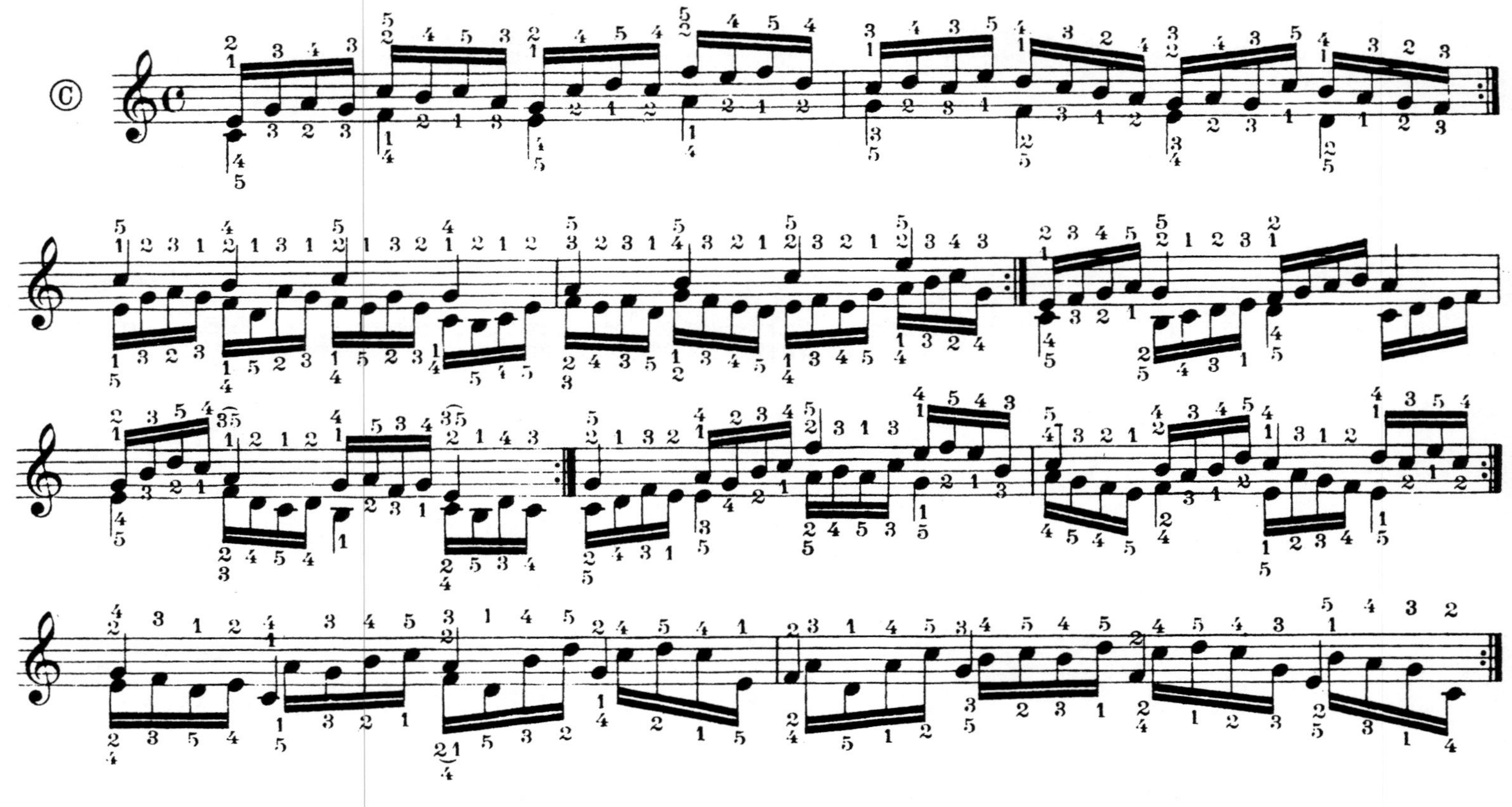

EXERCISE No 3d. *(2 notes against 3.)*

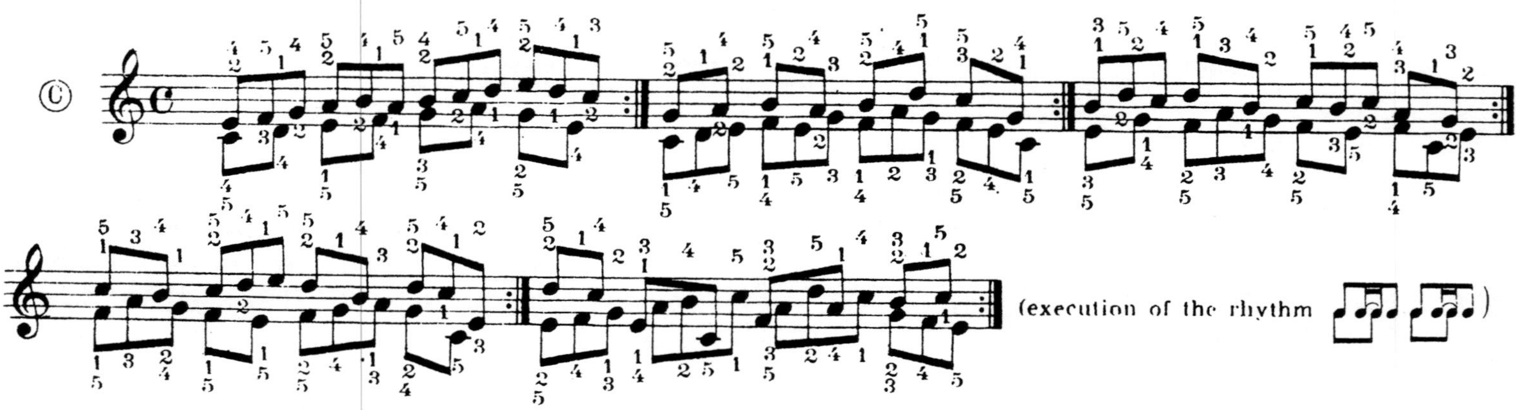

EXERCISE No 3e. *(3 notes against 4.)*

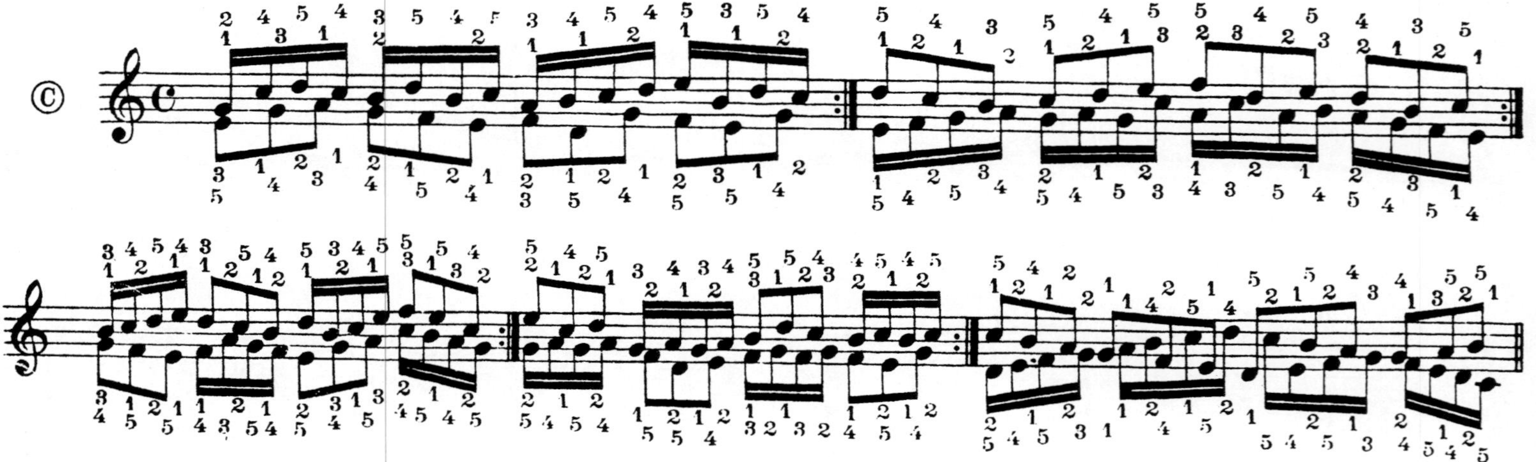

EXERCISE No 4. *(Three parts in different rhythms.)*

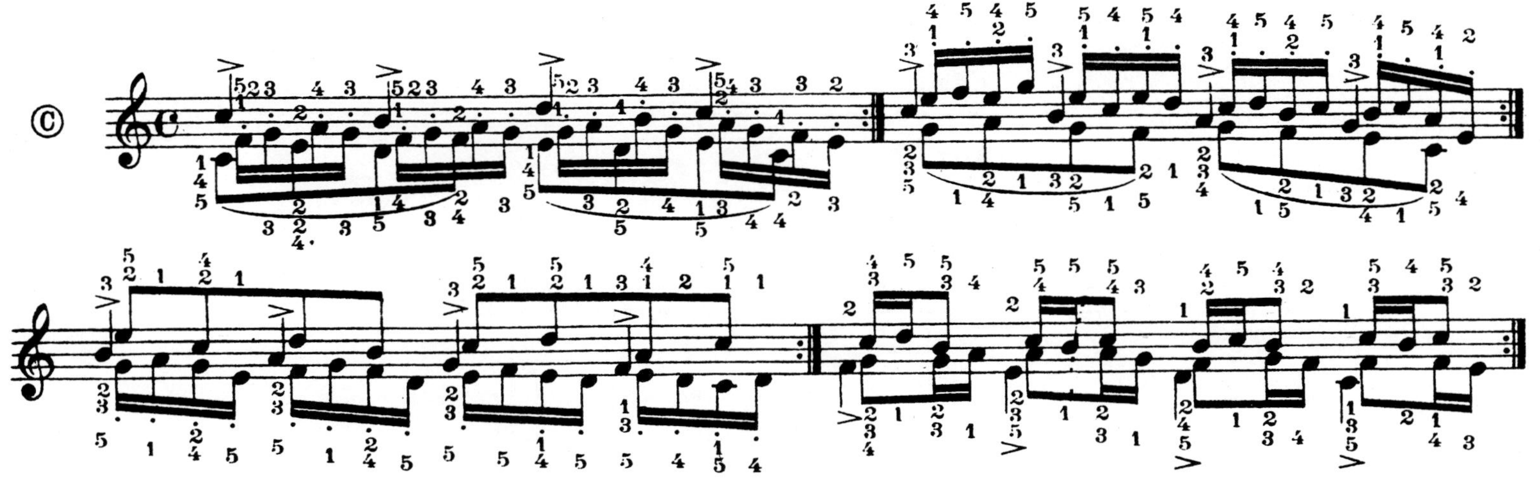

EXERCISE No 5a. *(In 2 parts with trill.)*

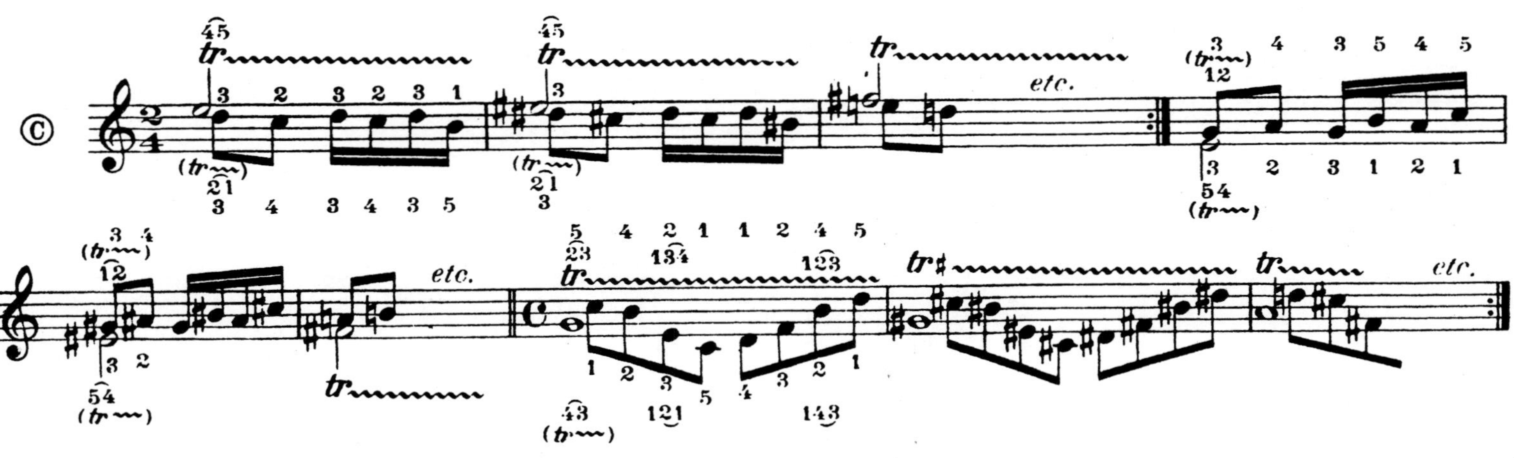

EXERCISE No 5b. *(In 3 parts with trill.)*

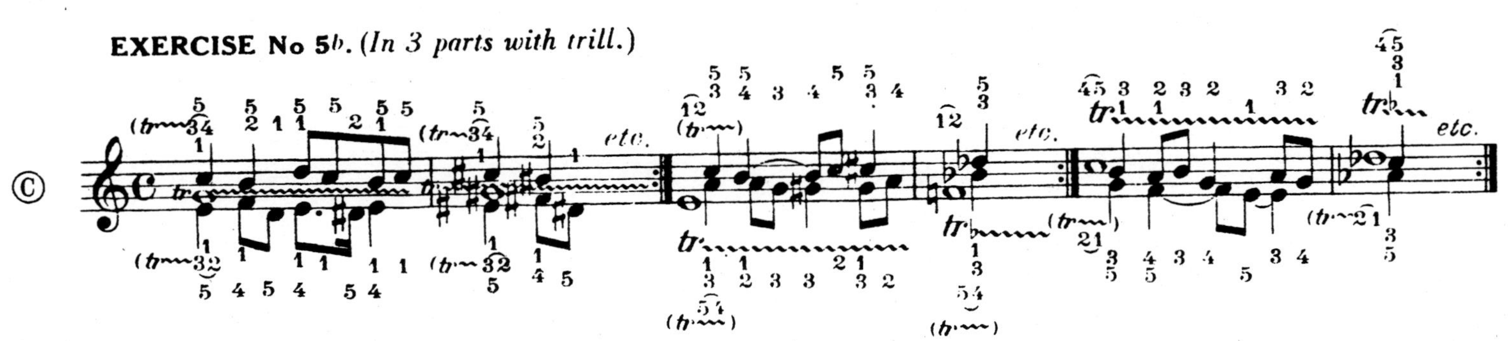

Complementary Formulae for Exercises

Composed by the Pupil or Recommended by the Teacher

CHAPTER IV

The technique of extension

It was only towards the end of the eighteenth century, when the pianoforte made its appearance, that the development of a wide stretch between the various fingers of one hand, became a problem in the technique of the key-board. The resources of the new instrument instigated explorations in a more copious harmonic style, and a more daring virtuosity than that of the harpsichord.

Until then the precepts for fingering in the old methods, were generally determined by considerations of convenience for the harmonization of figured-basses (1). Rare were the cases in which two neighbouring fingers had to execute an interval wider than a fourth, either in a chord progression or in the enunciation of a melodic design. The natural technical consequence of adopting a more widely spaced writing, such as the resounding faculties of the pianoforte invite, is the distension of the fingers, for their part is no longer limited to the rendering of the traditional cadences. Chords of the tenth and ninth become current. The very inflexions of melody frequently entail more extended skips, whose intervals have continued to increase up to the present day. Consequently we may assume today, that every pianist is obliged to have a stretch between two neighbouring fingers, at his disposal, whose angle exceeds the normal physical disposition. With the idea of correcting this limitation of the natural functions, which the needs of execution have by degrees changed into a positive defect, many systems of stretching have been adopted, both by exercise on the key-board, and by the most diverse mechanical devices. We need hardly add that the former of these are alone likely to give satisfactory results.

(1) The title of a work by Rameau "*Plan of a new method established on finger mechanics furnished by the fundamental succession of harmony*" clearly shows the preoccupation of the theorists of the time, on this subject.

But although they are less dangerous than the brutal distortions to which certain pianists are imprudent enough to subject their fingers, thanks to more or less complicated machinery, it does not follow that they can be recommended indiscriminately.

It is here that the teacher must take the conformation of his pupil's hand into consideration and direct his studies according to whether he belongs to the category of pianists with long or short fingers.

With this fact in view we have divided each series of exercises in this chapter, into two distinct sections, to suit each case respectively. We consider that, by conforming with this arrangement, recommended not by prudence alone. but it seems to us, also by logic, it may be confidently asserted that all such consequences as muscular fatigue or heavy execution will be avoided. These drawbacks are the usual results of thoughtless or too prolonged study of the technique of extensions.

SERIES A

EXERCISE No 1*a*. (*Progressive stretching of the fingers.*)

On the whole, it will be well to avoid extension exercises practised with a motionless hand, during which the fingers are cramped on the key-board in an abnormal position. They are nearly always fatal to muscular suppleness and often provoke serious accidents. Let us once more repeat that fatigue is the worst enemy of a rational training. The width of stretch between the fingers, should therefore only be practised progressively, without condemning the player to the useless torture of holding down the keys, and with a care for the constant suppleness of hand and wrist.

The normal stretch which it will be of use to attain between the fingers of one hand, must first be established. The limit of this extension is marked on the table below by the head of the arrow placed between the numbers of the two fingers affected.

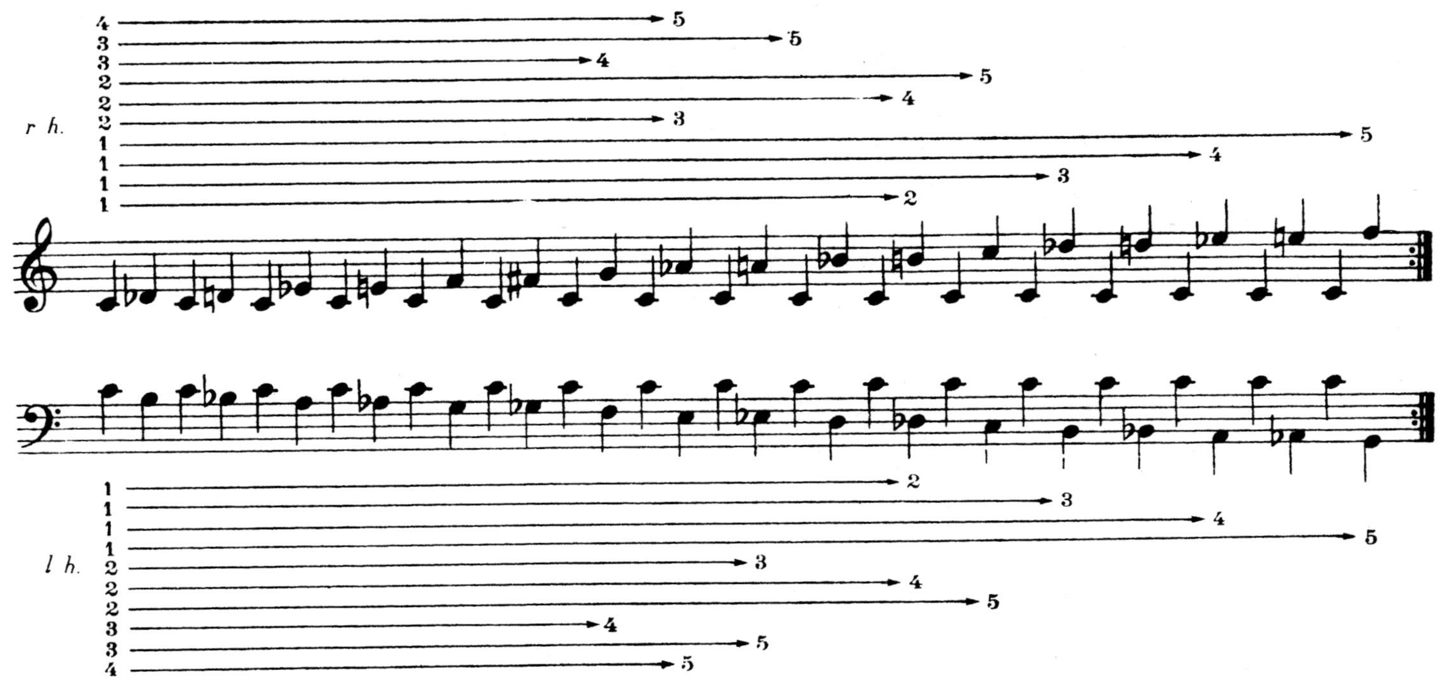

Only attempt to reach the maximum of extension between two fingers, after passing successively through all the intermediate degrees, according to the following example :

Example between 3rd and 4th fingers.

and so forth for all fingers.

In cases of difficulty in the execution of the widest extensions, accompany the movement of the fingers with a lateral rocking of the hand, which will facilitate the attack on each note. As far as is possible, avoid letting the attack fall on the side of the keys.

EXERCISE No 1*b*. (*This stretching exercise which we have already prescribed elsewhere (see commentary Nº 5 Students' Edition of Chopin's Preludes) differs from the preceding one, in that its action on the fingers executing the intervals is one of contrary motion. It is more effective, but also more fatiguing than the first. It must only be practised with great caution. The limits of extension to be attained between each finger naturally remain the same, as well as the fingerings: that of the left hand being naturally reversed.*

Do not try to hold both notes of the interval.

Merely observe the principles of legato, that is to say that each note should be linked to the next, practically as follows :

EXERCISE No 2a. (*Progressive formulae for extension between neighbouring fingers, for long fingered hands only.*)

The execution of notes extraneous to the strictly extensional formulae, has the salutary effect of relaxing the muscles of the fingers which have been momentarily subjected to the effort of a stretch. Practise each hand separately.

A. *between 1st and 2nd.*

Ⓒ Ⓡ *r. h.*

simile

idem.

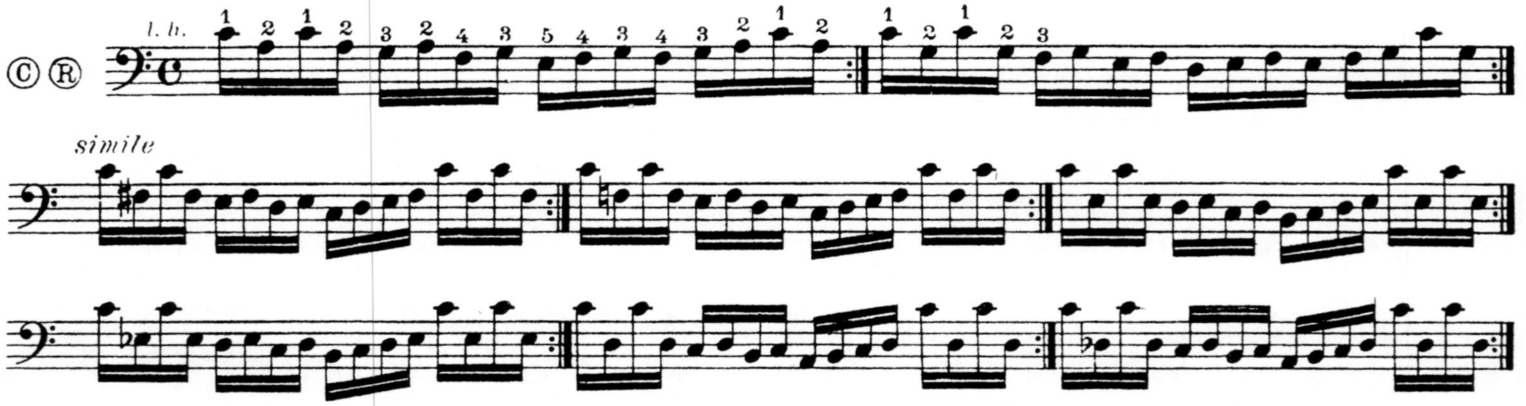

Ⓒ Ⓡ *l. h.*

simile

B. *between 2nd and 3rd.*

Ⓒ Ⓡ *r. h.*

simile

idem.

Ⓒ Ⓡ *l. h.*

simile

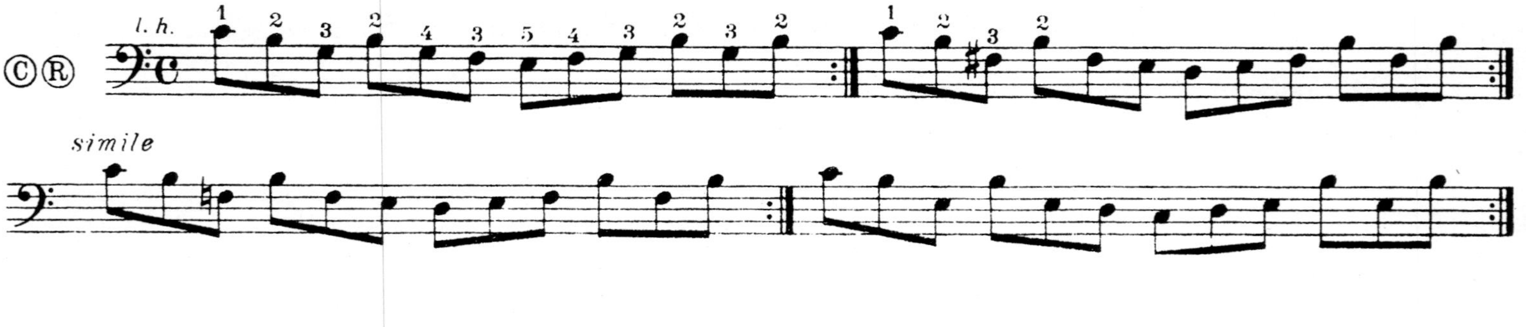

C. between 3rd and 4th.

B. between 2nd and 3rd.
r. h.
simile
idem.
l. h.
simile
C. between 3rd and 4th.
r. h.
simile
idem.
l. h.
simile
D. between 4th and 5th.
r. h.
simile
idem.
l. h.
simile
EXERCISE No 3. general distribution of extensions between all the fingers (long fingered hands.)
r. h.
simile
same formulae reversed, i. e.
etc.

EXERCISE No 3 *bis. same formula (short-fingered hands.)*

Each formula must first be studied separately, then in succession. In this last form, the finger movements are to be accompanied by a sort of rolling of the hand on the key-board, the wrist being held slightly higher than when in the normal position.

SERIES B

Extensions in doubles notes

Exercises Nos 2 and 3 of series A, chapter III will already have served as preparatory studies to the specialised examples which we give below. The difference which characterises the latter, apart from that of a more accentuated extension between the fingers, is the fact that they do not entail the passing under of the thumb, and that their object, if we may use this not very pleasing term, is the " dislocation " of the hand. The study of these exercises, and the same applies to all those contained in this chapter, must be carried out under the constant supervision of the teacher, who will decide on the number of daily repetitions for each one.

EXERCISE No 1. *(long-fingered hands.)*

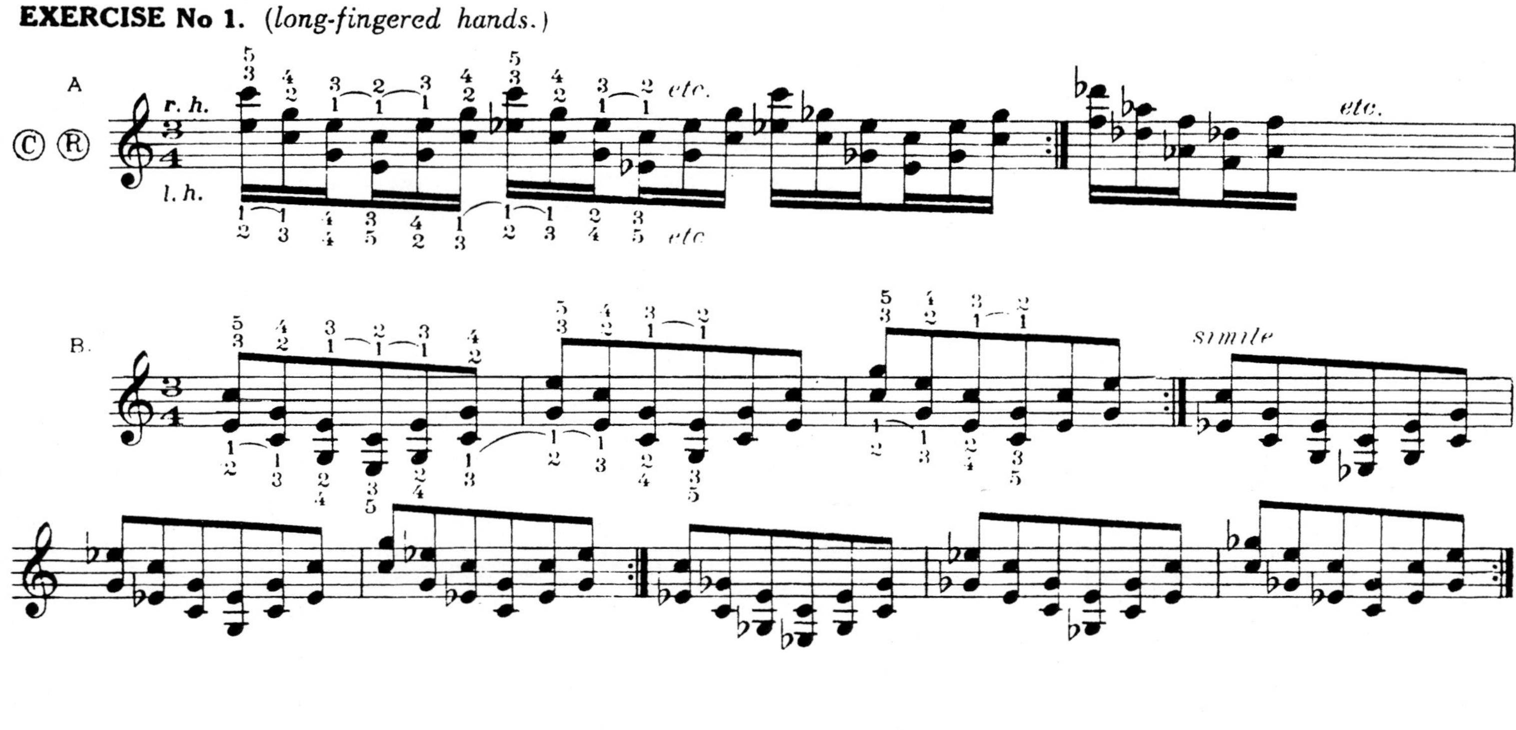

This mode of work is recommended even for short fingered hands, as a preliminary study indispensable to the following exercises.

EXERCISE No 2. *(extensions with tenuto.)*

A. *long-fingered hands.*

B. *short-fingered hands.*

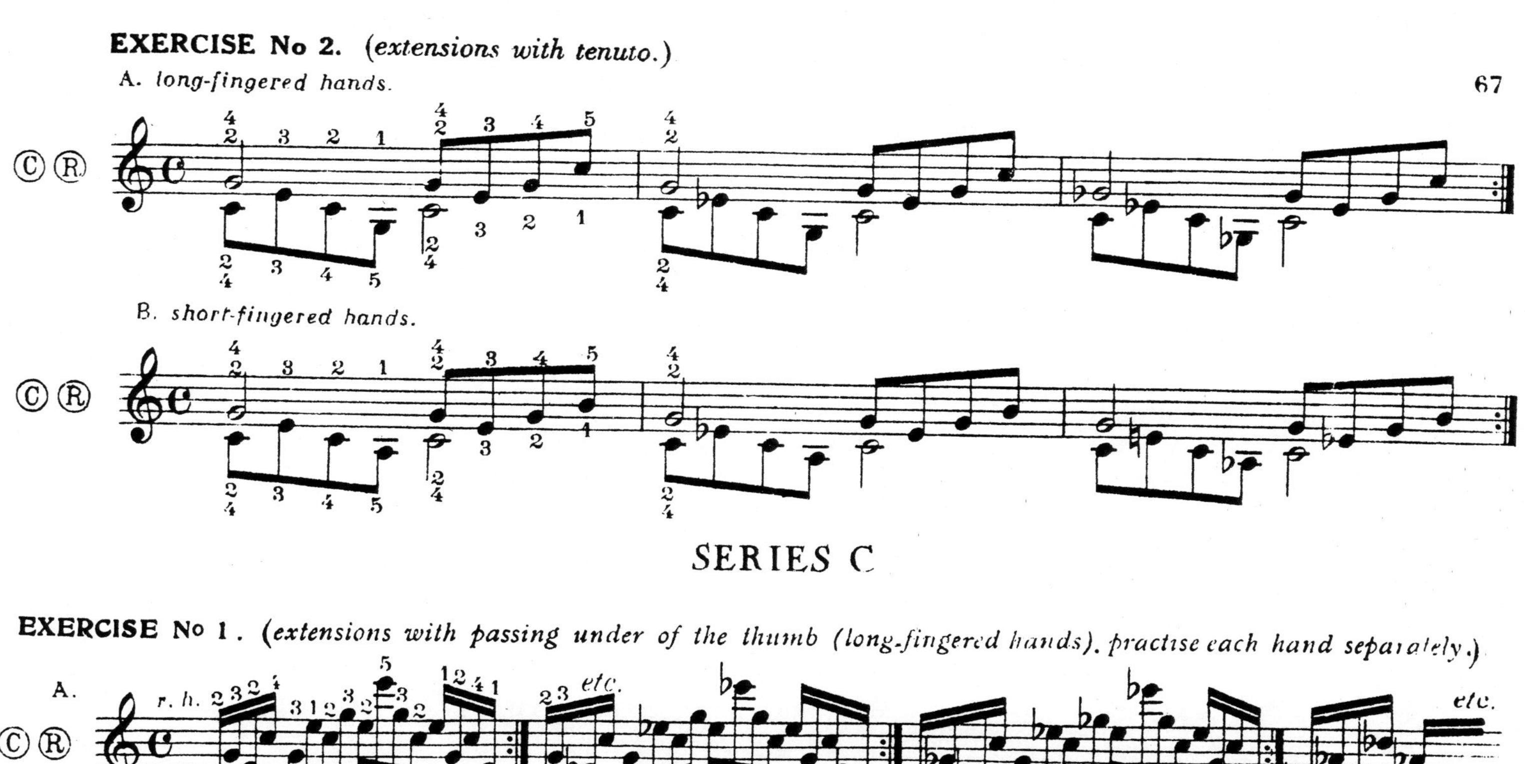

SERIES C

EXERCISE No 1. *(extensions with passing under of the thumb (long-fingered hands). practise each hand separately.)*

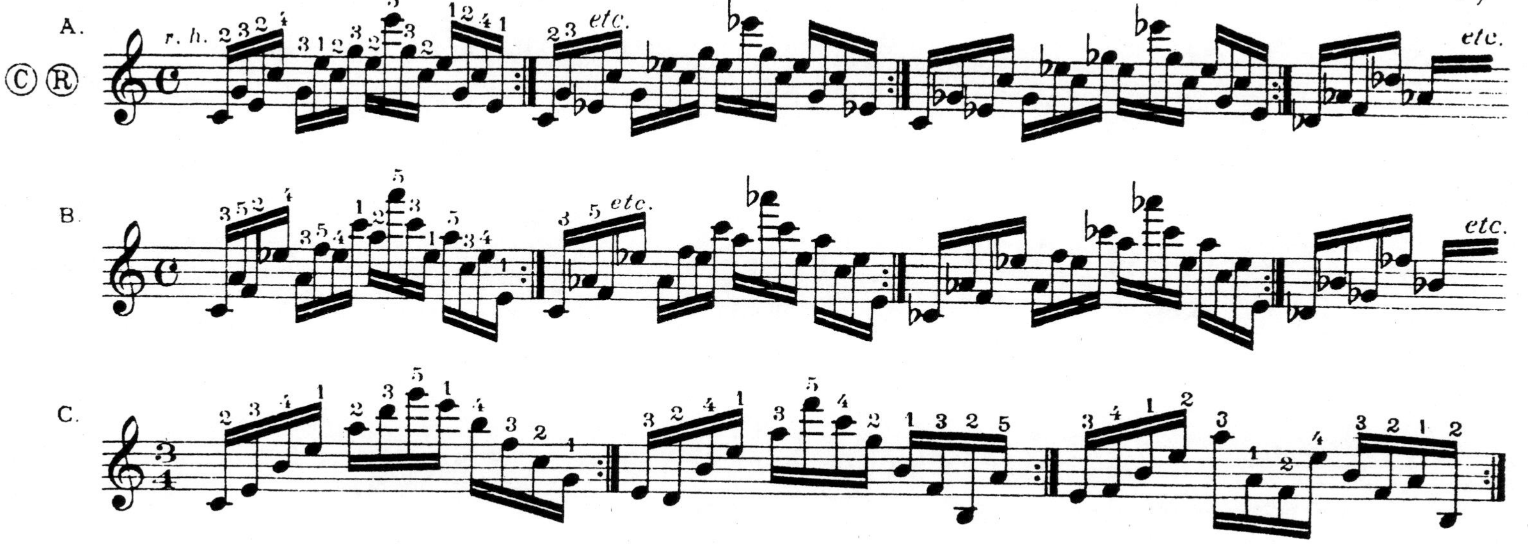

A.
r. h.
etc.
etc.
B.
etc.
etc.
C.

Special rhythmic variants.

additional to those contained in the table of rhythms

or

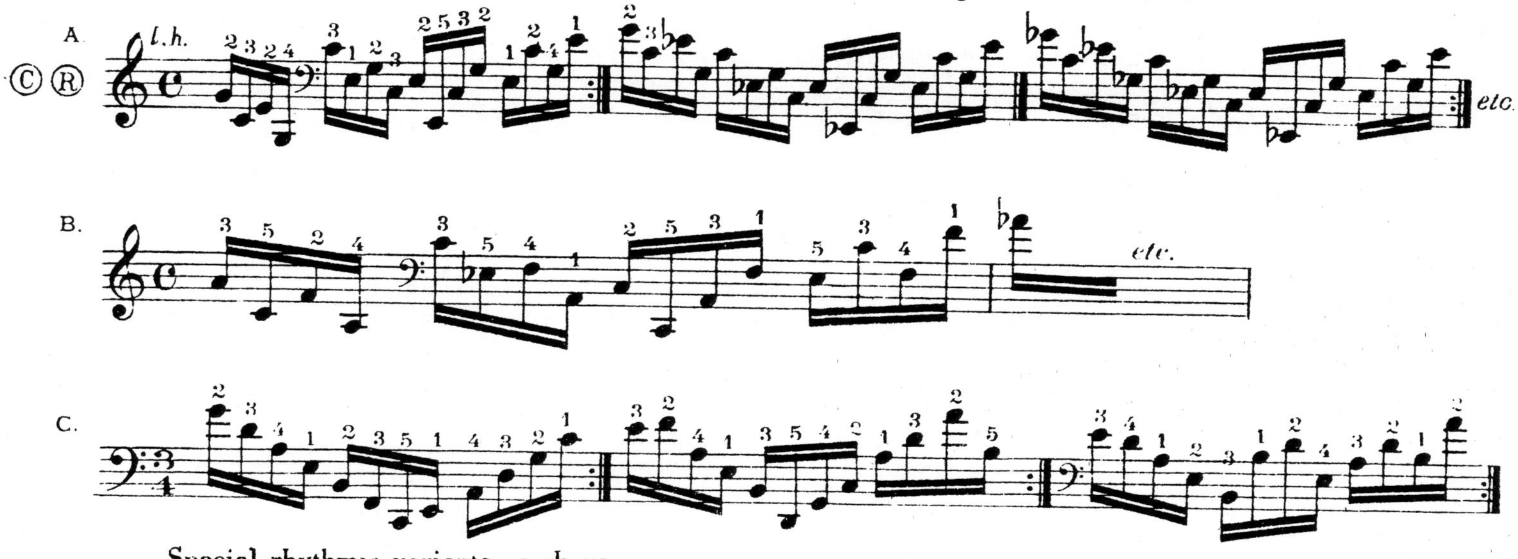

A.
l. h.
etc.
B.
etc.
C.

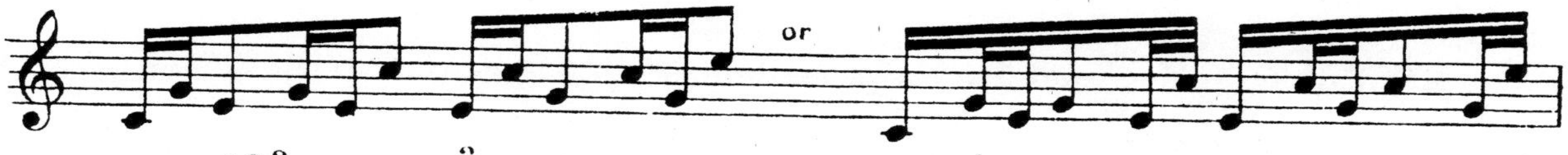

Special rhythmic variants as above.

EXERCISE No 1*bis. idem (short-fingered hands.)*

A.
r. h

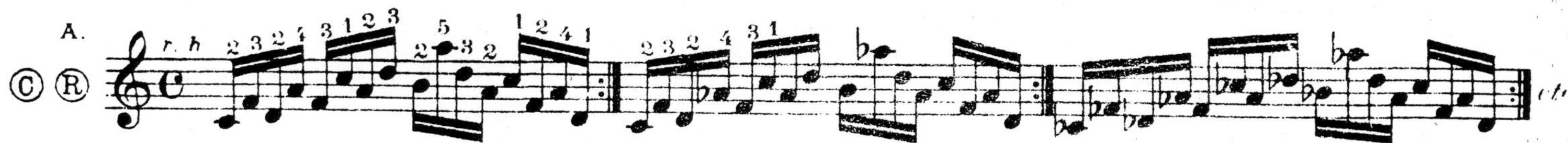

B.
etc
C.
Special rhythmic variants as above.
A.
l. h.
etc.
etc
B.
C.
Special rhythmic variants as above.
EXERCISE No 2. (extensions with substitution of fingers (long-fingered hands.)
with one finger held
etc.
etc.
etc.
with free hand
r. h.
simile
etc.
l. h.
etc.

EXERCISE No 2*bis*. *idem (short-fingered hands.)*

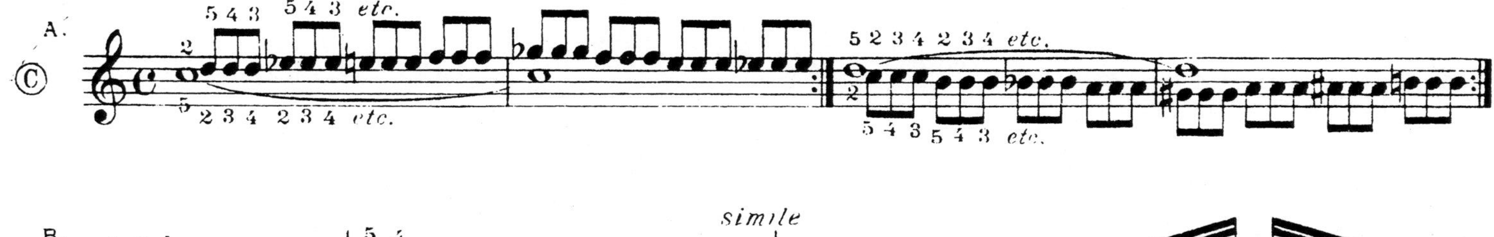

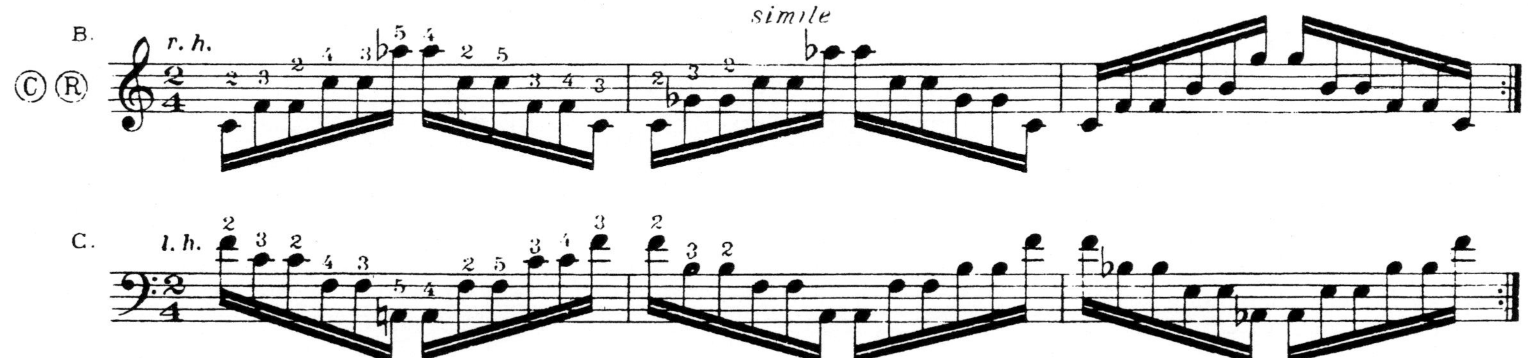

EXERCISE No 3. *(extensions between adjacent fingers in chromatic motion.)*

(long-fingered hands.)

(short fingered hands.)

EXERCISE No 4. *(extensions in chromatic motion between the fingers furthest apart.)*

A. *(long fingered hands.)*

B. *(short fingered hands.)*

Complementary Formulae for Exercises

Composed by the Pupil or Recommended by the Teacher

CHAPTER V

The technique of the wrist - The execution of Chords

The conclusion must not be drawn from the fact that we deal with the subject in the final chapter of this work, that the study of wrist movements only deserves a secondary place in the technique of the pianoforte.

Our idea, on the contrary, is that it ought to occupy the very first rank, when once the more elementary mechanical difficulties have been overcome, the schedule of which we have established above.

One is usually inclined, especially in the early stage of study, to trace all the merits of fine pianistic execution to a kind of purely digital dexterity. This conception moreover constitutes one of the well established principles of most didactic works. Since the tone of the instrument is produced by the concussion of the hammers on the strings, and since this concussion results from the action of the fingers upon the keys, it seems reasonable enough to conclude that the mobility and agility of the latter are the only important factors in the technique of the key-board. In reality, deprived of the help rendered to the fingers by flexibility of the wrist, this action has rather limited results. The degree of virtuosity to which one might aspire by devoting his essential studies to it, would not be of a very high order.

From a mechanical point of view, the conferring of mobility on the hand and fingers, presupposes the accompaniment of a parallel mobility of the wrist.

It is a widely spread error to think velocity of execution — that formidable ideal of pianistic studies — depends solely on the rapidity of movements of the fingers. In the execution of any passage requiring the displacement of the hand over several octaves (in fact in the whole literature of the pianoforte, excluding that of the harpsichord which is ruled by other technical conventions) the fingers are, in truth constrained to follow the impulsion given them by the wrist. To imagine that the hand should be carried along the key-board by the movement of the fingers is the equivalent of supposing that the wheels of a motor-car propel its engine.

It is impossible to appreciate the part played by the wrist in quality and gradation of tone, too highly. But this is speaking from the point view of musical interpretation, on which we regret not to be able to enlarge further, on account of the strictly technical nature of the present work.

We can find no better comparison for the action of the wrist than that of the violinist's bow. It is upon this that the thousand subtleties of punctuation and the most varied inflexions depend. The different degrees of weight which its various positions can communicate to the hand and consequently to the fingers, render it the true factor in sensitive and eloquent phrasing. It is therefore essential apart from the technique of octaves or staccato playing, both of which are entirely ruled by its action, to prepare the articulation of the wrist in such a way as to make it absolutely responsive, and to see to the suppleness of its movements, not only horizontally, following the plane of the keys, but also in its aspect of vertical rebounding.

We have endeavoured in the following pages to give some typical examples of this sphere of the wrist's activities.

We leave to the ingenuity of teachers or students, the care of developing its various issues, according to the peculiarities of each executant. Certain natural gifts facilitate the progress of wrist playing without apparent effort. Other cases of marked initial heaviness or stiffness, require on the contrary to be mastered by persevering work. We advise however that indiscriminately in both cases, the study hereafter indicated should be submitted to. For those who overcome these technical difficulties without effort, this work will only add to the development of one of the most precious resources of their future talent. Upon others, less favoured by nature, it imposes itself in the most peremptory fashion, as long as they are truly desirous of overcoming obstacles which would most surely keep them far from that pianistic perfection, which is the goal of their ambitions.

The technique of the wrist, - Horizontal movements - Vertical movements

The study of the different wrist movements required by pianistic execution can be simplified by being reduced to the following terms :

1. *Movements of horizontal propulsion.* From these are derived scales, arpeggios, glissandos and all leaps entailed by the execution of intervals exceeding the possibilities of extension of the hand.

2. *Movements of vertical propulsion* ensuring the repetition of the same chords or notes on the same keys, by the same fingers, allowing certain accents or attacks of special intensity. (Far be it from us, however, to dwell on manners of execution occasioned by the needs of musical expression.) These movements are also the basis of all kinds of staccato wrist playing, and of passages and trills played with alternating hands.

3. *Movements of combined propulsion*, that is to say, movements consisting of a series of actions on the part of the hand by which it is simultaneously displaced both laterally and vertically. These are used both for successions of chords or other notes, played by the same fingers on different degrees, and also for any sequence of chords composed of three or four simultaneously attacked notes, attaining or exceeding the interval of an octave.

4. *Movements of impulsion*, permitting of the execution of tremolando passages, of chords played arpeggiando, of broken chords, and of " batteries " in fact of all pianistic formulae requiring a more active participation of the hand than of the fingers as well as rebounding movements and displacements to and fro .

The first of the movements described above will be studied in Series A of this chapter, namely those of horizontal and vertical propulsion.

a) *Horizontal propulsion.*

The daily study of the chapter concerning key-board gymnastics will have made the fundamental principle of this movement familiar; see the preliminary exercise N° 9. But the variation which we propose here will allow of a less rudimentary application, and will make the use of this movement more comprehensible, in the rapid execution of all kinds of formulae entailing the displacement of the hand.

Let us mentally imagine an ordinary scale of three octaves, say the scale of C major. Ascend and descend this scale, striking one note only in each octave, while the fingers which should complete the rest of the octave perform their actions in the air and as rapidly as possible, having arranged their respective fingerings previously.

EXERCISE No 1.

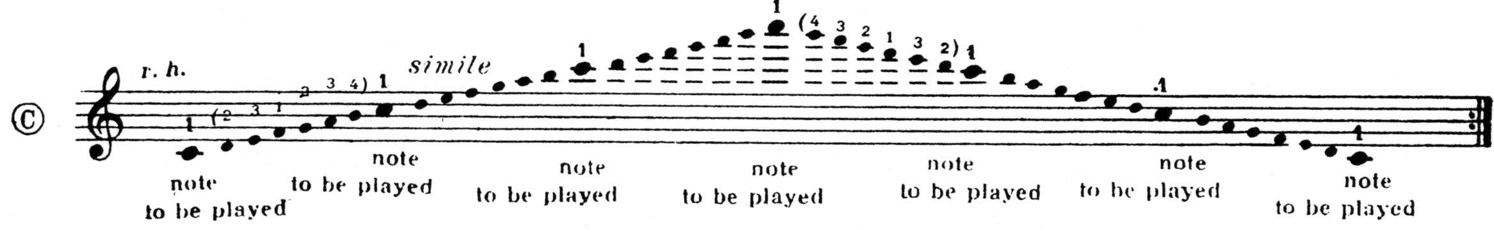

This will convey the idea of the exact part which the wrist should fulfil to assist in rapidity of execution, and it will thus be better understood, that in rapid virtuosity, it is the impulse of the hand which causes the fingers to advance and not the contrary.

Establish the point of departure of the " notes to be played " on each degree of the octave successively, adhering to the fingering of the scale chosen, whose key should be changed daily.

EXERCISE No 1*b*. *(same exercise on 5 octaves, playing one note in every other octave only.)*

The same formula applied to arpeggios and to chromatic scales, not merely by way of an incidental experiment, but as the object of a sustained study, will give the most conclusive results in the general amelioration of velocity, naturally both hands are to be practised according to this formula.

EXERCISE No 2 (*glissando*)

Glissando scales are played in two different ways, according to whether their execution be *f.* or *p.* In the first instance the phalanx of the thumb is generally used and poised almost flat upon the keys — or else the phalanx of the third finger stiffly straightened and turned over so as to present its outer surface to the key.

In *piano* the phalanx of the index or of the third finger is employed for preference, but in this case these fingers retain their natural position on the key-board. The hand need merely be inclined in the direction in which pressure is led, in order to sound the note, while the phalanx of the finger in action fulfils the role of the quill on the cog-wheel used in games of chance.

The position of the wrist also differs according to the case. In *forte* the wrist is turned over outright with its back to the keys : it draws the hand along in ascending, and in descending the scale it precedes it; in *piano* it pushes it along, both going up and coming down. In both cases the wrist has entire command of the execution, the hand and fingers remaining passive. The study of Glissando should be commenced *piano*, and at first restrained to the practice of limited intervals, whose extent should be gradually increased. The key of C major is naturally the only one to be employed for the study of these exercises.

EXERCISE No 2*a*. (*glissando p.*)

Make a distinct pause on each point of departure and of arrival in the scale. Employ all the fingers in turn. Alternately practise the sliding notes as though unstringing beads, that is to say in an almost slow tempo, and again in a rapid movement evoking the idea of a rocket of sound.

EXERCISE No 2*b*. (*glissando f.*)

For glissando *Forte*, two octaves must be employed in continuous succession.

Change the finger on the final note.

Give strong accent to the first and last notes of each scale. Work in a brisk tempo with great decision in the movements of the wrist.

EXERCISE No 2*c*. (*Glissando in double notes*)

The position of the hand and fingers in double note Glissando, differs according to whether the scales are in thirds, fourths, sixths or octaves. Scales in thirds or fourths are played like single Glissando executed piano, when the hand is pushed along by the wrist. For scales in sixths and octaves, the fingering generally employed thumb and fifth finger) entails a special position. In ascending the lowering of the keys is effected by the fifth finger-nail, and the lateral surface of the thumb's smaller phalanx; in descending, it is effected by the outer surface of this phalanx and the extremity of the small phalanx of the fifth finger.

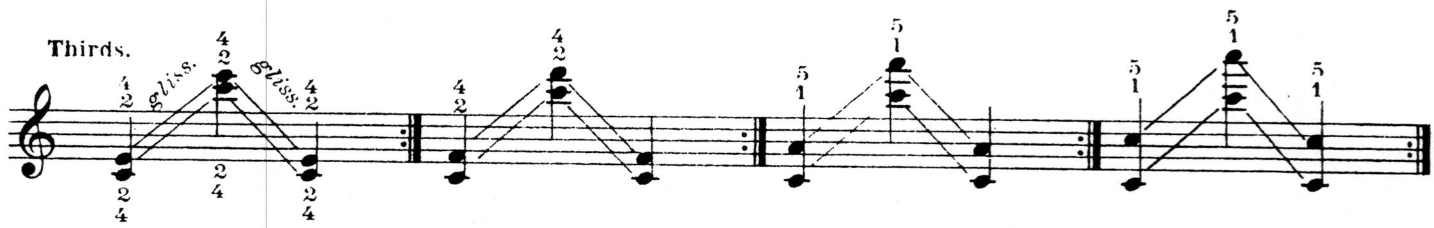

EXERCISE No 2d *(Glissando on black keys)*

For Glissando on the black keys, the usual mode of execution consists in using, for the right hand in ascending motion and the left in descending, the external extremities of the third and fourth fingers held firmly together and outstretched; the wrist is turned oyer, as in single Glissando executed *forte.*

In descending with the right hand and in ascending with the left, the internal extremities of the same fingers, in the same elongated position, are used, and the wrist regains its normal position.

EXERCISE No 3. *(Leaps)*

Leaps are of two distinct types: one, that which is effected by skimming the key-board, in order to bridge the space separating two distant notes or intervals; the other, that in which the wrist causes the hand to describe a more or less accentuated curve in order to carry it from one note or interval to another. The first is not unlike a kind of mute Glissando of which the first and last note only would be heard. It is employed for preference, when the first note of the interval is shorter than the second :

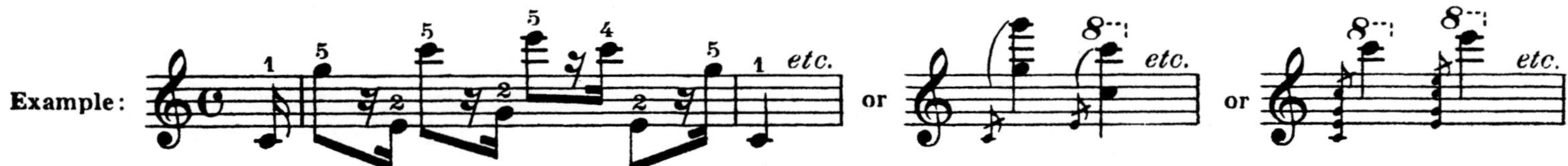

or also when for an interval of reduced size, two neighbouring fingers, or even the same one, are used with a rapid movement :

The leap with a curve is especially suited to the linking together of two distant intervals, so that during the kind of trajectory performed by the hand over the keys as it travels from one point to the other, the fingers are enabled to prepare their position for the clear enunciation of the interval at which they are aiming.

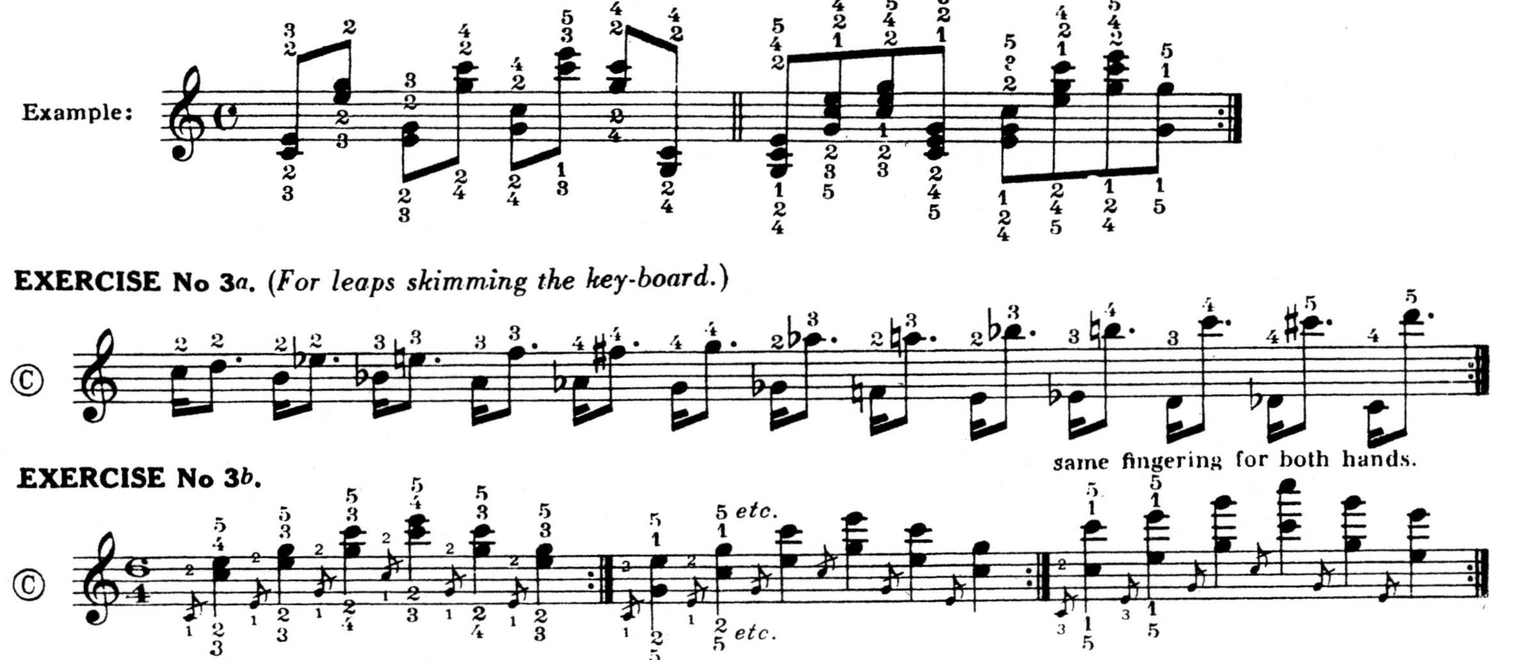

EXERCISE No 3a. *(For leaps skimming the key-board.)*

EXERCISE No 3b.

Practise this exercise on the following minor and diminished intervals also :

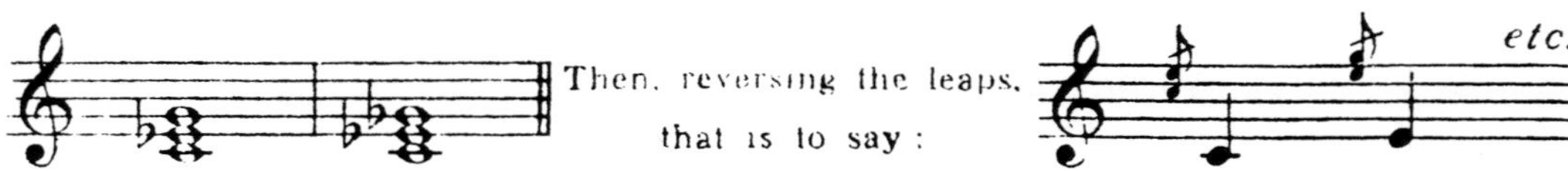

EXERCISE No 3c. (*For leaps with curve; vary the fingerings.*)

Employ the same formula for leaps in chromatic succession, adding all the intervals up to the octave inclusively.

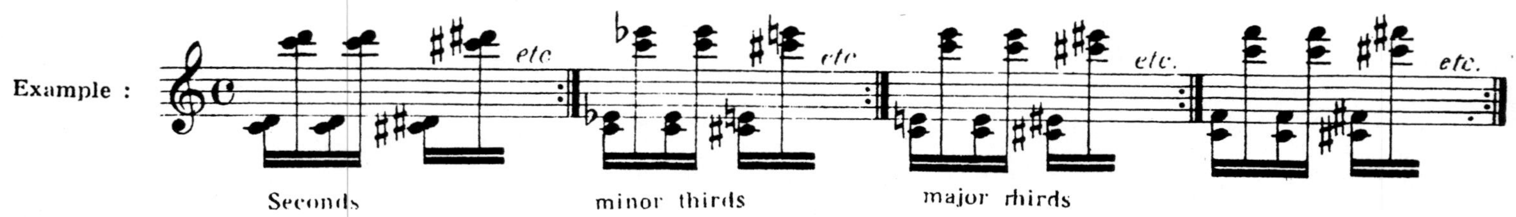

During the study of curved leaps, take care that, in the middle of its trajectory, the hand passes at about the height of the shoulder, and that the wrist describes its elliptical movement with suppleness and decision.

Crossing Hands

The passing of one hand across the other entails a different wrist mechanism according to whether it is effected over or under the hand.

In the first case the trajectory is rounded, in the second, it skims the keys as closely as possible.

These two modes of execution are to be applied successively in the following exercises, which can be studied indiscriminately by either hand.

A. (*one hand motionless*)

B. (*Contrery movements in both hands.*)

C. (*Arpeggio formulae in ascending motion.*)

D. (*Idem. Descending motion.*)

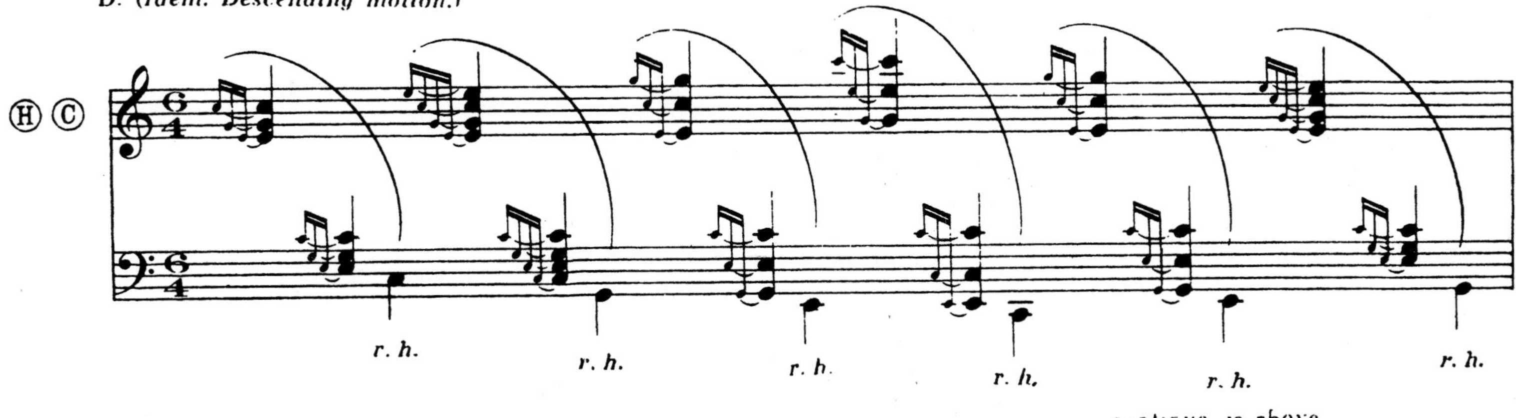

B. *Vertical propulsion*

Preparatory exercise for the analysis of the movement.

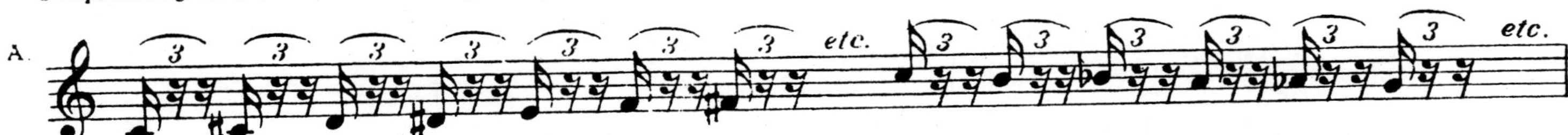

Count one, two, three, on each triplet. One — to strike the note dropping the hand on the key-board with rapidity, suppleness and decision; two—to continue the movement of the hand below the key-board, lightly touching the knee, which is taken as a resting point ; three — to bring back the hand to the position of attack, that is, at about the height of the shoulder. During this exercise the wrist must be in a constant state of suppleness as well as the hand. The finger used to strike the key, must alone be firm at the moment of playing.

Employ on this chromatic succession all the fingers and all chords of two notes, successively.

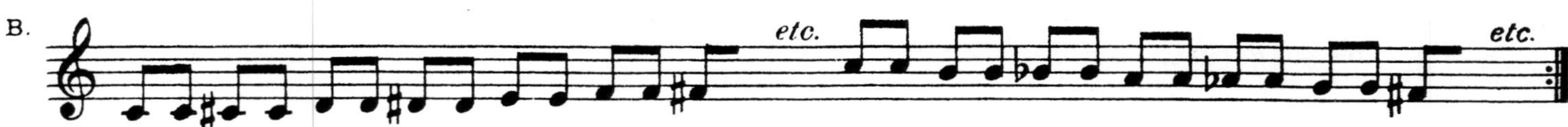

In this exercise the movement of the hand is not to be prolonged below the key-board, but after playing each note the wrist should be brought back to the height of the shoulder. To be practised as above.

EXERCISE No 1. *(For vertical attack and firmness of the fingers; to be played slowly only.)*

Make a large and pronounced movement for each attack, letting the wrist rebound to the height of the shoulder after each note.

The position of the fingers must be prepared in the air before each change of chord.

The movement of vertical propulsion is specially suitable to the execution of octaves or of detached chords in playing *forte* and in a slow or moderate tempo; which allows the hand to recover its elevated position of attack before each stroke.

In a succession of this kind, for instance.

EXERCISE No 2 *(For the execution of detached octaves and chords.)*

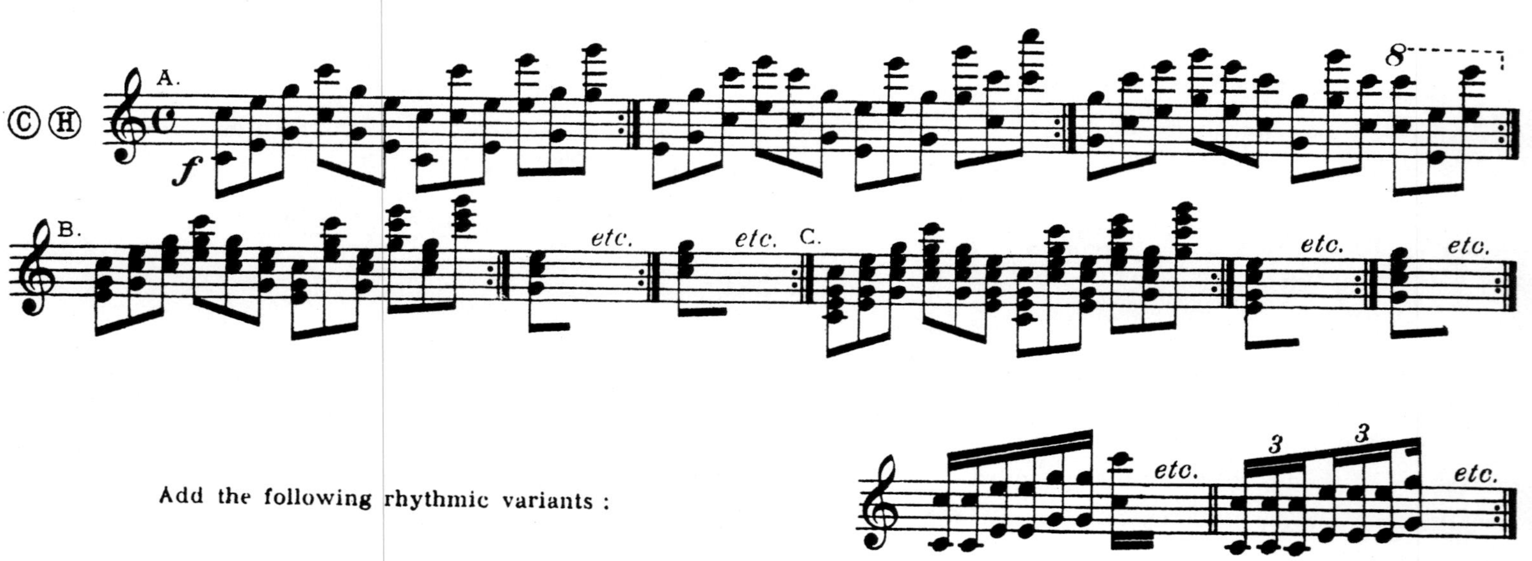

Add the following rhythmic variants :

EXERCISE No 3

The attack or the finish of a brilliant passage is often accompanied by a movement of vertical propulsion, with the object of re-inforcing the tone of the essential notes. Practise the following formulae, attacking the initial note from a height :

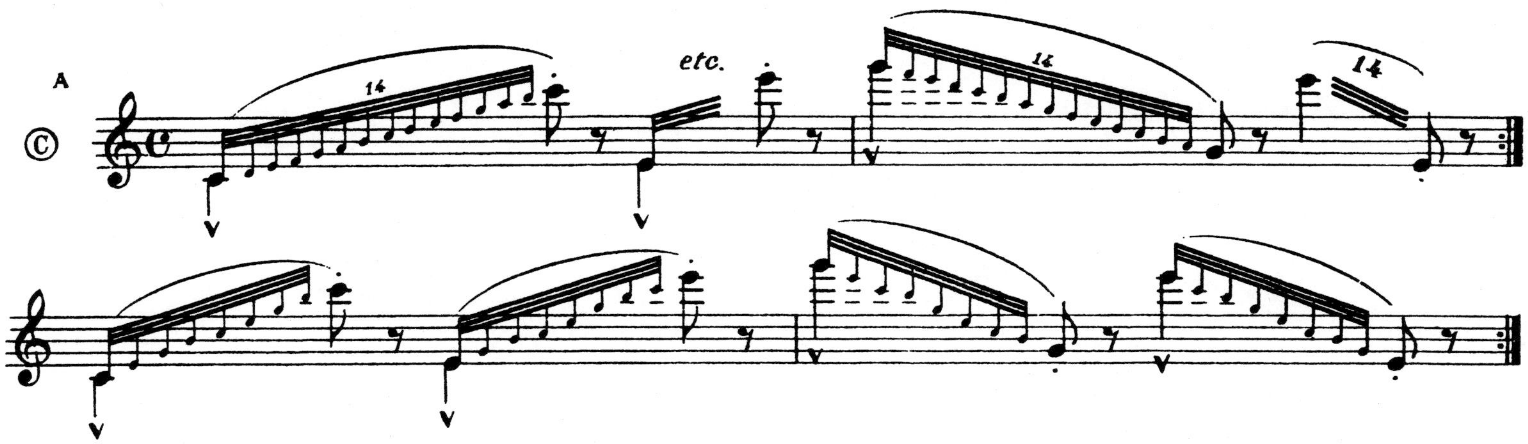

B. The comma corresponds to the vertical raising of the hand to prepare the attack of the crotchet.

EXERCISE No 4. (*Alternating hands*)

The technique of alternating hands depends first and foremost, on vertical propulsion. Absolute regularity of execution, is, in this case, based on a corresponding equality in the amplitude of the wrist movements, which cause the alternate attacks of each hand to succeed one another on one or several notes.

First practise on a single note according to the following rhythmic formula :

A. *Repeated notes* (Employ each finger in turn.)

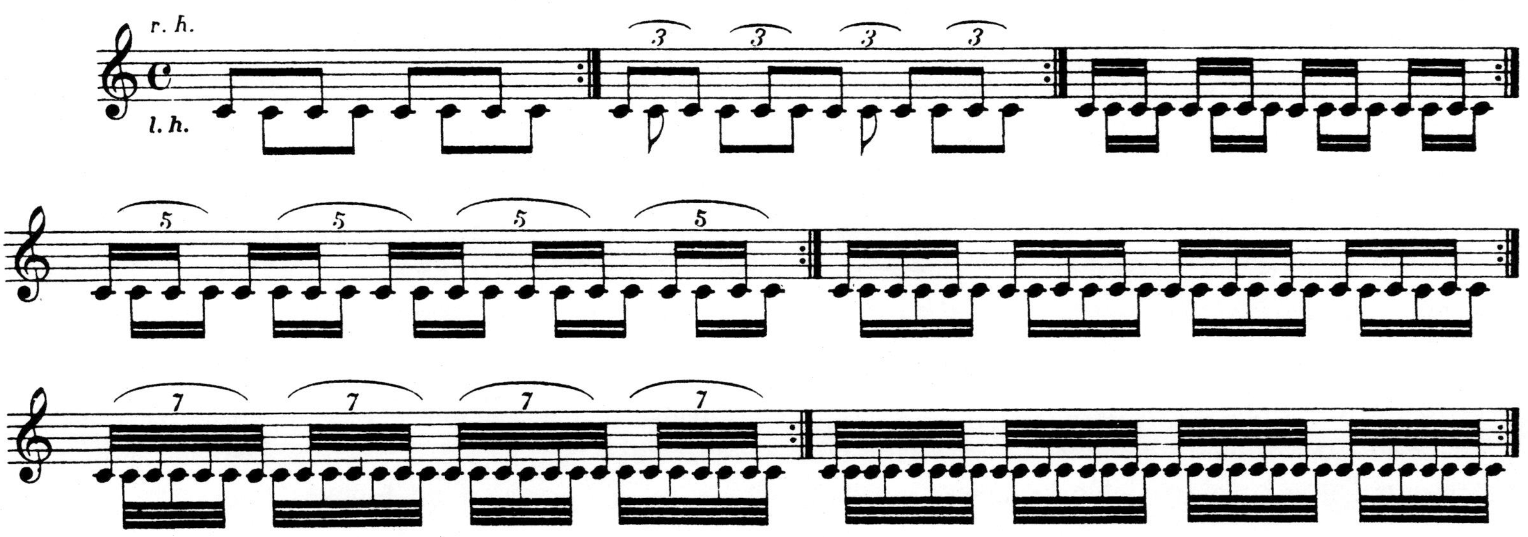

Throw the hands alternately on to the selected key, taking the point of departure for each attack at the height of the shoulder. As the rhythm accelerates, gradually diminish the height of the attack, whose point of departure must, however, remain absolutely symmetrical in both hands.

B. *Trills or Percussions.*

Same rhythmical formula as above, but on various intervals.

C. *Scales and Alternating Passages.*

To be developed over several octaves.

D. *Chromatic Scales.*

Beginning with the left hand.

Beginning with the right hand.

(Use all fingers and all rhythms.)

Formulae to be developed over several octaves.

All the preceding exercises are to be studied using all the fingers successively.

It will be sufficient to add to each of the notes of the above exercises, taking them as bass notes, intervals of seconds, thirds, fourths, and sixths, to give rise to an entirely new series of formulae, permitting the study of double notes in alternate hands.

Examples.

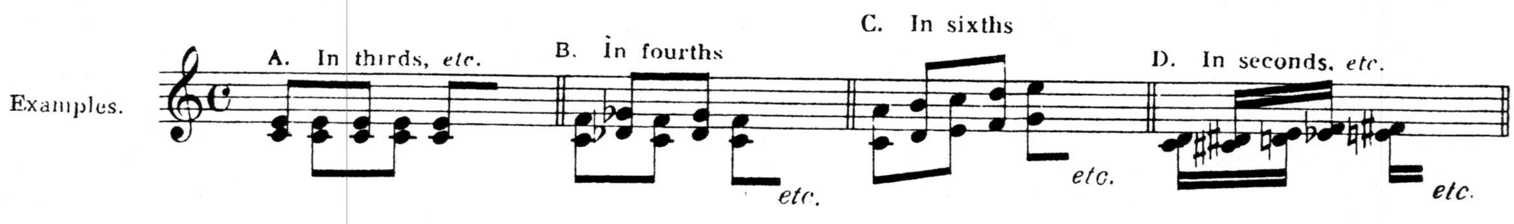

EXERCISE No 5 *(Alternate octaves)*

The technique of alternate octaves is characterised by this fact, that it is only the two thumbs which succeed one another on the same plane, thus establishing the intermediary part in a succession. All the formulae in Ex. N° 4 are to be practised in the following way :

Examples

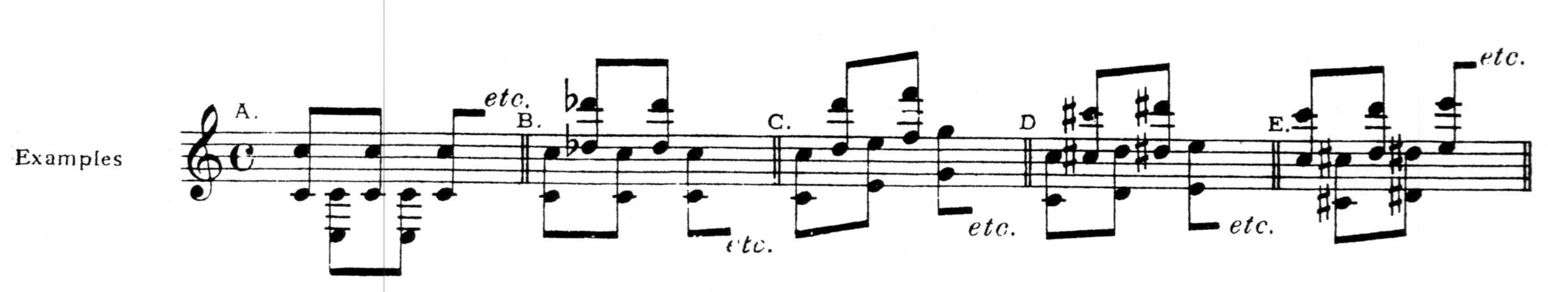

EXERCISE No 6 *(Passages shared by both hands.)*

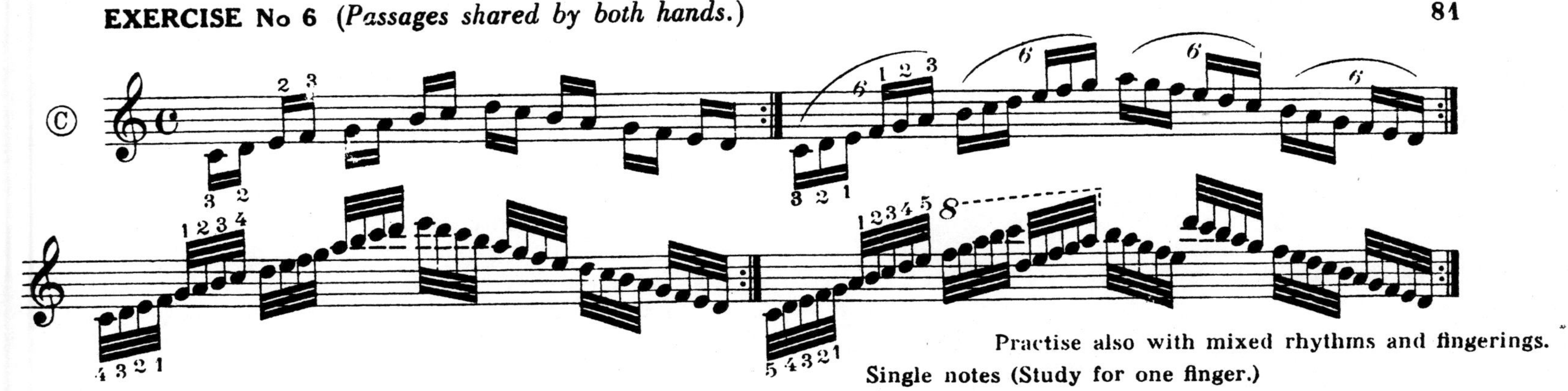

SERIES B

Movements of combined propulsion

Combined lateral and vertical displacements

(As the vertical attacking impulse is given to the first note of each group, the fingers, afterwards, merely skim the keys.)

A. Movements of combined propulsion. Simultaneous lateral and vertical displacement.

EXERCISE No 1 *(Successions of notes executed by the same fingers on different degrees : formulae to be extended.)*

(to be practised by both hands)

The above examples have been established by taking into account the almost traditional formulae which most frequently recur to the fingers in the execution of successions of octaves or consonant chords. It is by practising every finger in turn on each series of notes, that the fundamental technique of the following exercises ir which these formulae are used, will be most efficaciously prepared.

EXERCISE No 2. *(Double notes and chords.)*

Since progressions of chords executed by one hand can only come under one or other of the following headings :

1° { *lower part in motion* / *upper part motionless*

2° { *upper part in motion* / *lower part motionless*

3° { *inner part in motion* / *outer parts motionless*

4° { *outer parts in motion* / *inner parts motionless*

5° { *all parts in motion*

It will be sufficient for us to suggest one model for each heading, for which variations will be supplied by the application of the table of harmonic combinations.

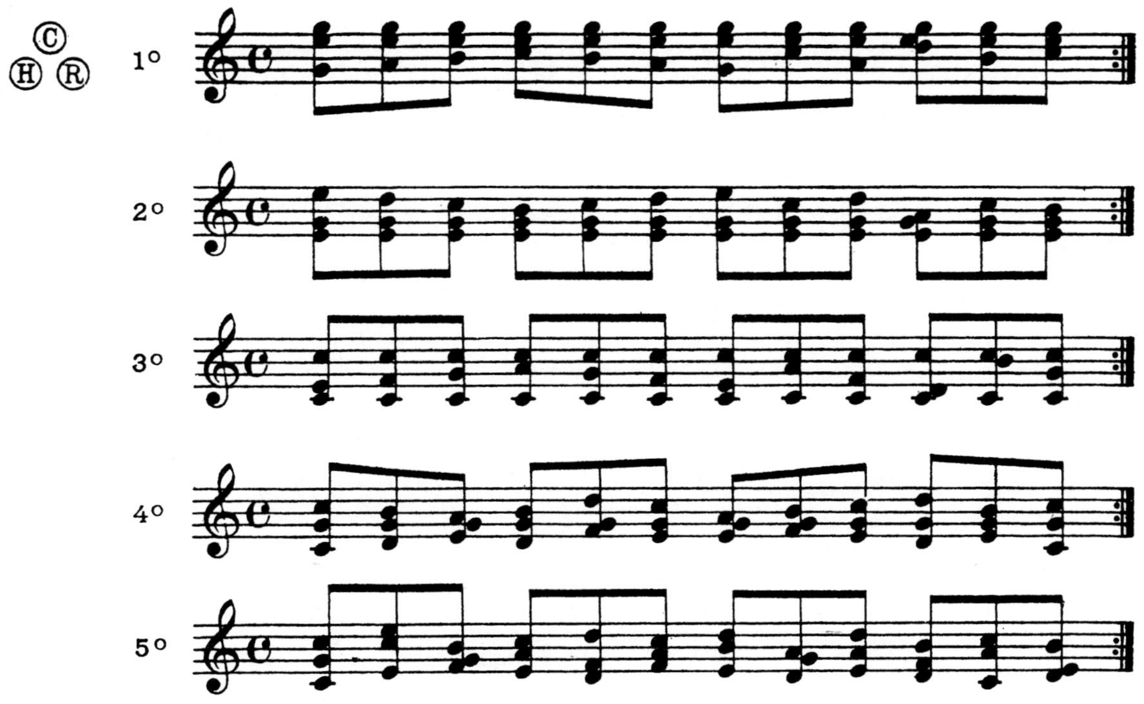

(To be practised on chord formations of four and five notes also, inspired by the same formulae.)

EXERCISE No 3*a* (*Single tremolo*)

The single tremolo is nothing more nor less than a trill whose position is widened. But instead of being produced by alternate articulation it is generally subordinate to a movement to and fro on the part of the wrist; this, in rapid execution, ends by being merely a sort of trembling which communicates itself to the fingers. Its mechanism will be better understood, by practising slowly the following progressive rhythmic formula.

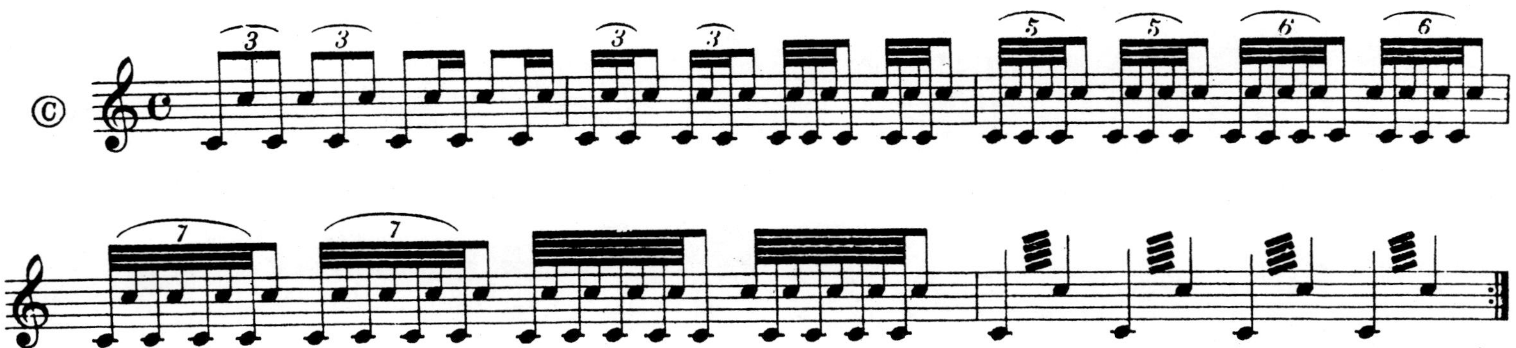

Repeat this exercise beginning with the upper note so as to invert the position of the fingers on the different rhythms. Practice also on the intervals of the fourth, fifth, sixth and seventh.

EXERCISE No 3b *(Stationary tremolo)*

The preceding observations can equally be applied to the double tremolo which might be described as "a trill of chords". Except for certain special positions such as

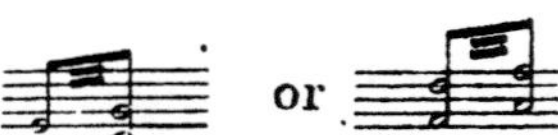

which require the articulated participation of fingers, it is executed in the same way, and is to be practised on the same rhythmic model according to the following formulae :

Also practise the inversions of these positions, as well as the harmonic variants provided by the examples (H) in the transferable table.

EXERCISE No 3c *(Tremolo with displacement of the hand.)*

Also practise beginning with the upper note.

Same formula with the following formations.

EXERCISE No 4. *(Open chords)*

In the execution of certain open chords the role enacted by the fingers is an almost passive one. It is restricted to preparing on the key-board the position of the notes to be played, and it is a movement of semi-rotation of the wrist which brings about the emission of sound. The greater the number of notes contained in a chord and the more extended its position, the more justifiable is the use of this movement.

Models of open chords to be executed by rolling the hand.

EXERCISE No 5 *(Broken Chords)*

The rocking motion of the wrist equally facilitates the execution of broken chords in double notes passing from one octave to another. In this case, however, the fingers must remain firm and must not give way to the alluring tendency of an arpeggiando emission of the simultaneous notes.

Taking the following models as a basis, this special study can, if deemed necessary, be intensified as this form of virtuosity sometimes incurs unforseen physical resistance.

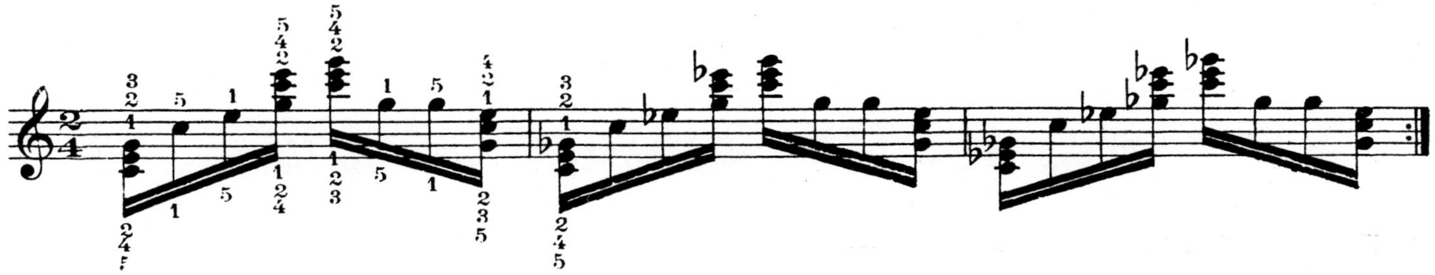

EXERCISE No 5*bis* *(Broken chords in scale form)*

Though their execution seems at first to depend on a form of lateral propulsion, the simultaneousness of attack of two or three notes will only be obtained by means of a vertical movement of the hand allowing the fingers to fall perpendicularly on the keys.

Employ the same formulae on the chromatic scale.

EXERCISE No 6 *(Batteries.)*

This name does not only serve to designate a now obsolete form of accompaniment, equally known under the nomenclature of Alberti's bass.

It also specifies the pianistic process consisting of a kind of measured tremolo, one of whose parts moves melodically on different degrees, while the other acts as a pedal by a continuous repetition of the same note.

In extended positions, the fingers are powerless to mark the melodic contour of the moving part with the necessary agility and force. In this case the intervention of the wrist becomes necessary for clearness of enunciation. It is manifested by a succession of rocking movements on the part of the hand, whose amplitude varies in proportion to the width of the intervals; each swing corresponds to a characteristic attack of the finger or fingers in action.

EXERCISE No 7 *(Rebounding on the same notes with the same fingers.)*

This formula differs from the example given in the preceding series, in so far that the movement of propulsion instead of being given on each note or chord is common to a group of repeated notes. The first spring must therefore be sufficiently pronounced to cause the hand to rebound upon the keys in a series of as many bounces (which imperceptibly sink towards the depth of the keyboard) as there are values to be executed in each group.

EXERCISE No 8

The substitution of fingers on chords generally brings that flexion of the wrist into play which we have elsewhere described as the " drawer movement ". It consists in facilitating the change of fingers by means of the successive advancing and withdrawal of the hand on the keyboard.

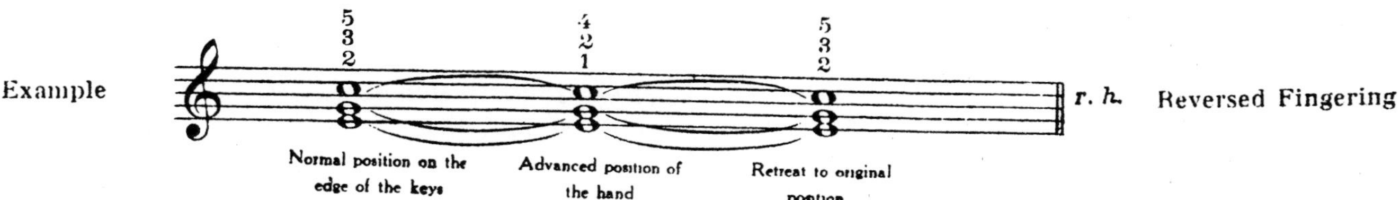

This mechanism which is easily understood in a slow movement, becomes more complicated in rapid execution. Its assimilation is to be prepared by the study of the following formulae in legato substitution.

Vary the rhythms of the substitutions without repeating the bass notes. The same work for the left hand, with the fingering reversed.

B. *Articulate substitutions.*

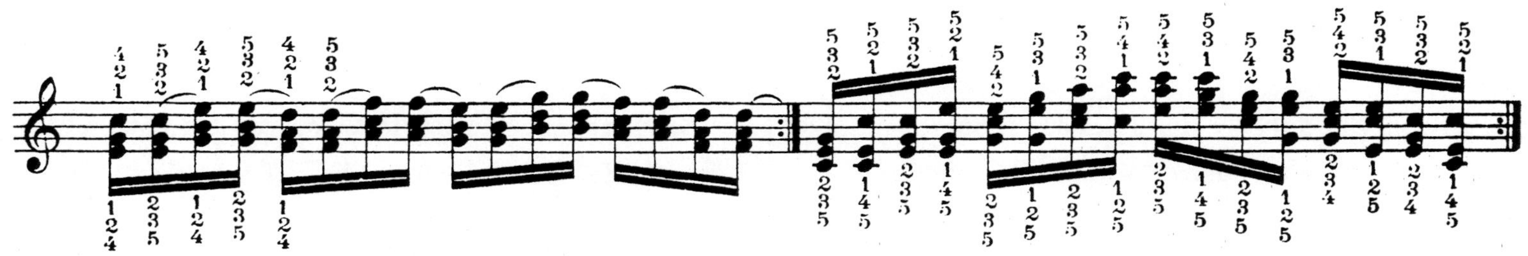

C. *Syncopated substitution.*

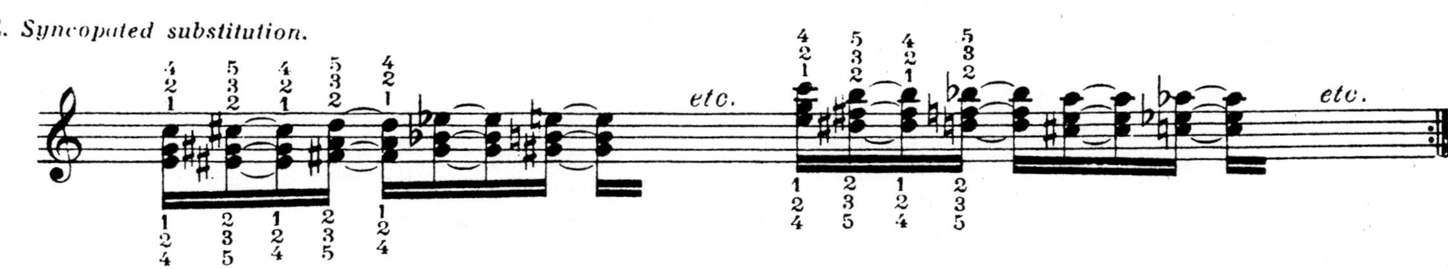

SERIES C

The technique of octaves

The utility of suppleness in the movements of the wrist, for the execution of octaves, is a fact so obvious that we feel no need to insist upon it. But we should like to try and establish the factors by which the mechanism of this movement, comparatively simple in the case of detached octaves, differs and becomes complicated when it is associated with the action of the fingers; an action which, practically non-existent in the execution of detached octaves, is, on the contrary, of extreme importance in the case of octaves executed legato.

It seems to us that the movements of the wrists necessitated by a perfect legato execution of octaves can be divided into three categories.

1. The movement of suspension, that is to say, the alternate raising and lowering of the wrist, without letting the fingers which play the octaves leave their keys.

2. The backward and forward movement from the white to the black keys and vice versa.

3. The movement of lateral displacement in ascending or descending motion.

Strictly speaking, the movements of the first category are not absolutely indispensable for the legato execution of octaves.

No interpreter, however, in possession of a slightly refined technique, fails to employ them, almost unconsciously. We shall therefore attempt to demonstrate their use and define the conditions of their application.

In octaves, legato playing is necessarily fictitious, since it is a material impossibility for the thumb to insure an uninterrupted continuity of tone between the various notes in its part.

Only the illusion of it can be created, and this is achieved by conferring a slight predominance of tone on that part of the octave which can be fingered, and which, consequently, is really capable of being bound.

Now this way of playing imposes a muscular constraint upon the executant, which is contrary to his natural physical abilities, since it requires a greater expenditure of strength on the part of the weaker fingers than from the thumb, which is admittedly the strongest.

It is here that the movements of wrist suspension intervene; these, since they enable the executant to distribute the weight of the hand among the different fingers at will, thus make it possible for him to counter-balance their inequality, to increase the powers of resistance of the third, fourth and fifth fingers, and on the contrary, to lighten the action of the thumb, while preserving its suppleness and mobility; in fact, to co-ordinate, in a single supple and easy gesture, muscular efforts of a contradictory nature.

A. Movements for loosening the wrist.

First practise these movements on a single held octave, counting *one* to lower the wrist, *two* to raise it.

EXERCISE No 1*a*

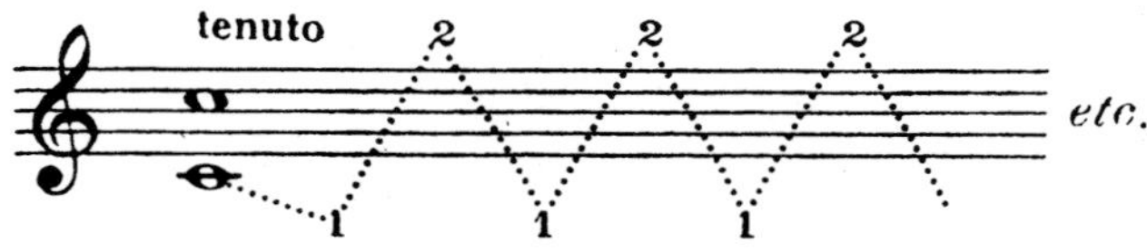

To be repeated twenty times, gradually increasing the rapidity of these movements without diminishing their amplitude.

Afterwards practise holding one of the notes of the octave only, letting the repetition of the other co-incide with the lowering of the wrist.

EXERCISE No 1*b*.

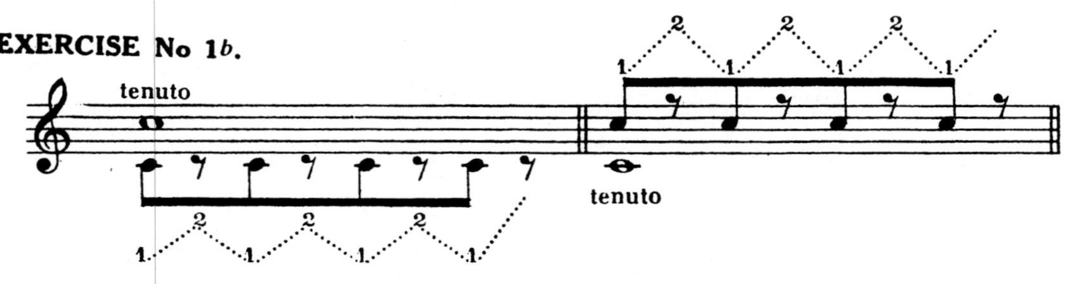

Then start linking the octaves together, applying to them the principle of hand movement described above, and playing the part confided to the weak fingers, strictly legato.

EXERCISE No 1c.

Invert this formula for the left hand.

This formula is gradually to be extended to groups of octaves whose number should be increased little by little, until a diatonic scale has been established, whose length should, for the present, be limited to one octave.

Examples :

EXERCISE No 1d.

The scales are to be played, in a moderate tempo.

EXERCISE No 1e.

Continue the preceding work (scales of one octave only) stressing the preponderance of tone in the outer voices of both hands and introducing the principle of repetition of the thumb into this exercise, so as to develop the mobility of this member.

Let the attack of the thumb always coincide with the lowering of the wrist .

Lateral action of the thumb :

EXERCISE No 1*f* *Legato of the outer parts of both hands.* (*Reverse the position for the left hand.*)

Having attained flexibility in the movements of the wrist in the preceding exercises, practise the other voices legato (upper voice in the right hand and lower voice in the left) in the following way.:

Invert this exercise for the practice of the left hand.

B. " *Drawer movements* ". These facilitate the displacement of the hand in passing from the black keys to the white, and vice versa; and, in the latter case, allow the thumb to slide from one to the other, thus ensuring an almost perfect legato in both voices.

They must first be practised by dividing the advancing movement towards the back of key-board, or the movement of retreat to the initial position, into a series of small displacements on the same keys.

EXERCISE No 2*a*

corresponds to the following positions of the fingers on the keyboard; the figures indicate the successive positions, in each octave of the fingers on the keys.

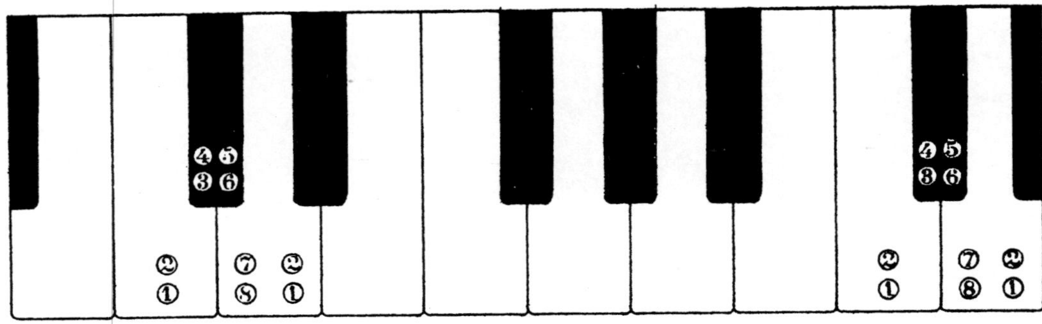

Let the fingers advance or recoil by means of a very slight but precise movement of the wrist, while the hand remains supple. Practise disjunct intervals from black to white and from white to black keys in the same way, without exceding the interval of an augmented fourtn between two consecutive octaves.

EXERCISE No 2*b*.

Accelerate the movement progressively. As the rapidity increases, gradually loosen the successive relaxations of the wrist, in such a way as to reduce the action to a single perfectly rounded gesture.

EXERCISE No 2c *(Trills or shakes in irregular rhythm.)*

Increase the interval between the octaves up to the minor sixth.

EXERCISE No 2d. *(repeated octaves.)*

Since the so-called " drawer movements " maintain the suppleness of the wrist, their use is especially satisfactory in long passages of repeated octaves. They make it possible to execute these with a minimum of fatigue, while the vertical propulsion or the nervous contraction, of which certain pianists make use, rapidly cause a sensation of weariness and effort.

First study according to the rhythmic formula of exercise N° 2c.

So as to become familiar with the advance and retreat of the fingers on the keys. Then repeat each of the following models twenty times, practising one of them each day on different degrees.

EXERCISE No 2e. *(Study of chromatic successions in octaves, with sliding fingers in both voices.)*

Same fingering reversed for the left hand, as the sliding takes place on the same degrees.

Lateral displacement of the wrist.

EXERCISE No 3a *(Broken chords in succession.)*

The mechanism of this displacement will be accentuated and therefore rendered more comprehensible by the preliminary study of the following exercises in broken octaves.

In a general way the two variants given above should be applied to all the exercises in octaves contained in this chapter. Their efficacy will be especially felt in the study of formulae in disjunct motion.

EXERCISE No 3b (*Incurved or turning movements.*)

The impulse given by the wrist at the moment of passing from ascending to descending motion, or inversely, must proceed from a supple but absolutely neat and unhesitating gesture.

The fingers must remain in close contact with the keyboard. They must, so to speak, skim the keys even in the execution of the most distant intervals.

The theoretical principles of the movements for loosening the wrist having been well established (1), by means of exercises whose study requires care and attention at least equal to that given to the preceding chapters, practical formulae for the execution of octaves legato can now be approached. First practise scales and arpeggios according to the models previously indicated for single notes.

(1) In this theory of the execution of octaves we have made extensive use of the commentary in our Student's Edition of Chopin's Studies (Study No 10, Op. 25)

EXERCISE No 4a. (*Scales.*)

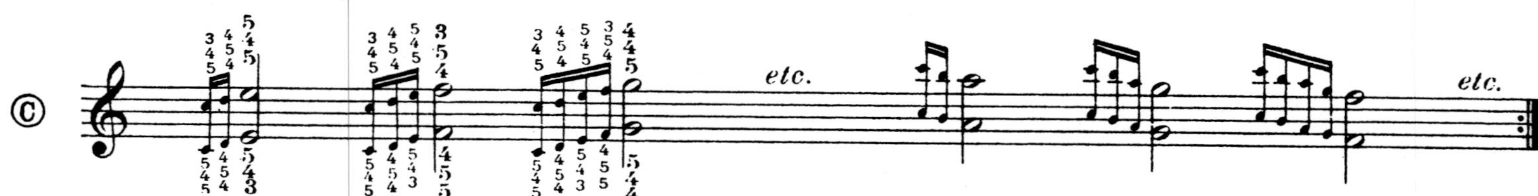

Then scales with all fingerings, in all major and minor keys, over a space of three octaves, alternately legato and staccato; and in contrary motion.

EXERCISE No 4b. (*Chromatic Scales.*)

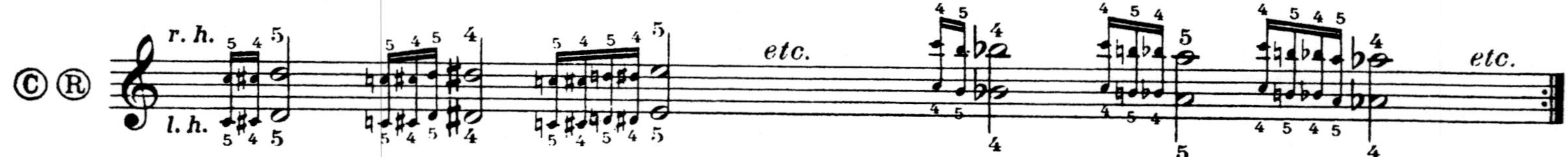

Practise the chromatic scale, taking a different starting point on a different degree each day; and also in contrary motion.

EXERCISE No 4c. (*Arpeggios.*)

EXERCISE No 4d. (*To ensure legato in the outer voices.*)

Next practice ordinary arpeggios (perfect chords, chords of the seventh and of the ninth) with the variations of the rhythmic table which is to be generally employed for all the formulae throughout this exercise.

EXERCISE No 5

We give below some traditional patterns of passages in octaves, the musical " padding ", as it were, of pianistic rhetoric. By the application of the variations of rhythm and transposition from the transferable table, by the extension of their scope on the key-board, taken alternately legato and staccato, they will be transformed into the most efficacious exercises, and their study will make a very sure preparation for the execution of numerous pianistic writings contained in the repertory.

A. *Passages in octaves with both hands in parallel motion.*

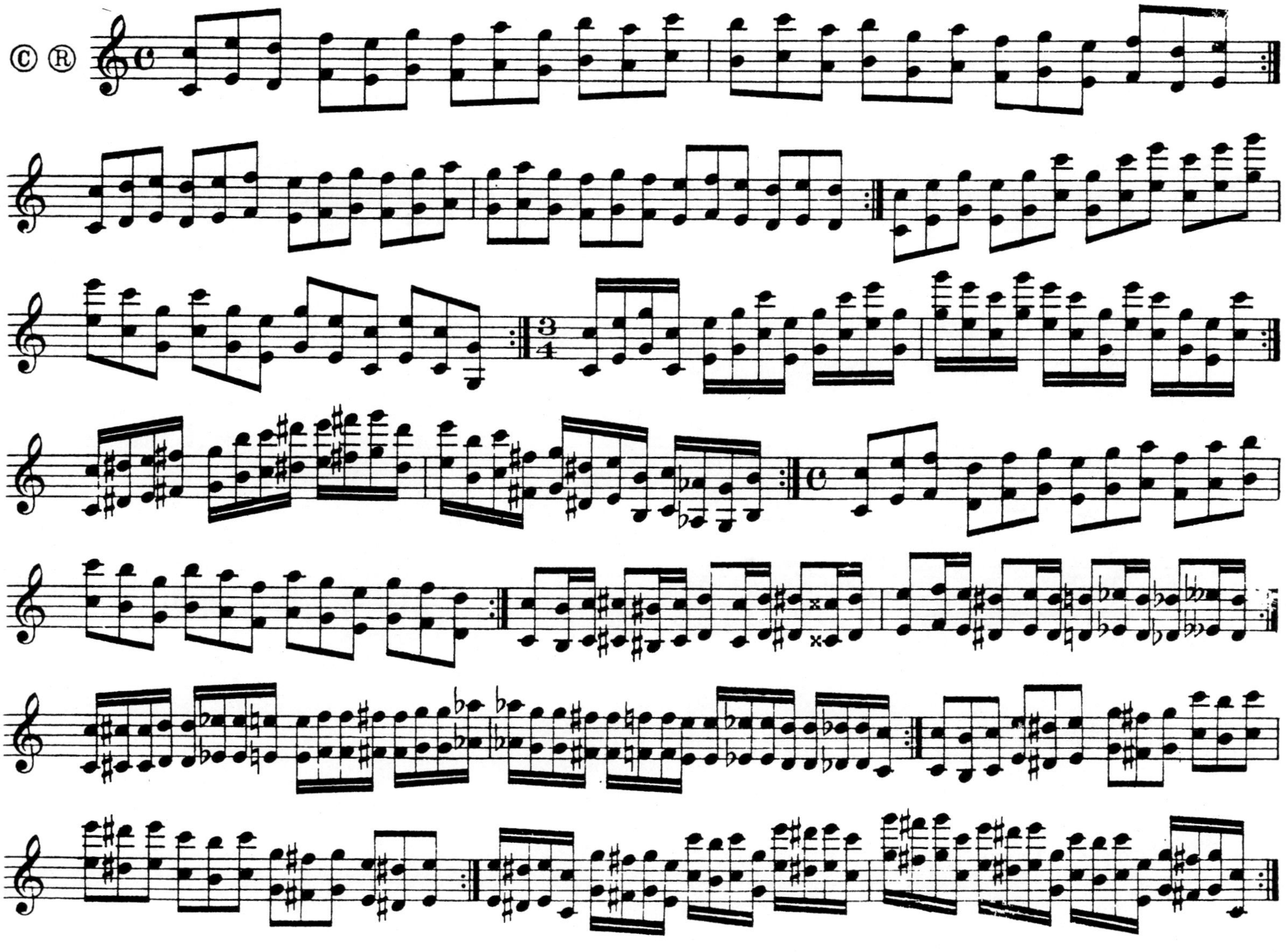

to be studied successively legato and staccato and with different fingerings.

B. *Passages in octaves with both hands in contrary motion.*

Complementary Formulae for Exercises

Composed by the Pupil or Recommended by the Teacher

REPERTORY

There can be no question of mentioning here all those classical works, whose musical value is backed by a special technical interest, and to which the study of this collection of exercises might serve as a complement or a preparation. We have only be able to include those compositions, a knowledge of which is indispensable to anyone undertaking classical pianistic studies.

We leave the completion of this repertory to the care of the teacher, according to the requirements of his pupils. We do not think it necessary to recommend the works of Clementi, Czerny, Cramer, Kessler, etc..., to him. No serious musical education could be complete without them.

The degree of difficulty of every piece is indicated opposite the names of the works, in the column corresponding to each chapter, in the following manner :

N. D., not difficult - R. D., rather difficult - D., difficult - V. D., very difficult.

It will be well not to forget in referring to these qualifications that, in the perfect interpretation of a musical work, it is not the number of notes contained in it which constitutes its real difficulty. As far as we are concerned, we consider the execution of an « andante » by Mozart or of a Bach Fugue as a higher token of virtuosity than that of a Liszt Rhapsody.

Let us here recall the various subjects treated in the five chapters of the work

Chapter 1. — *Equality, independence and mobility of fingers.*
— 2. — *Passing under of the thumb (scales, arpeggios).*
— 3. — *Double notes and polyphonic playing.*
— 4. — *Extensions.*
— 5. — *Wrist technique, execution of chords.*

In cases of works containing technical peculiarities which cause them to depend on several chapters, the degrees of difficulty are marked in the columns alloted to the chapters dealing with those peculiarities.

1. - The Harpsichord

ITALIAN SCHOOL

G. FRESCOBALDI 1587-1654?

	Chapters				
	1	2	3	4	5
La Frescobalda (expressive polyphonic playing)			nd		
Partita sopra " L'Aria della Romanesca " (variations)	nd		rd		
Partita sopra " La Monica " (idem)	nd		rd		
Toccata in G. Minor (evenness, polyphonic playing)	d		rd		

B. PASQUINI 1637-1710

	1	2	3	4	5
Toccata sul Canto del Cuculo (evenness, lightness)	d				

A. SCARLATTI 1659-1725

	1	2	3	4	5
Toccata in G. Minor (evenness, polyphonic playing)	rd		nd		
Toccata in A. Major —	d		td		

DOM. SCARLATTI 1685-1757?

(Scarlatti's pieces for the harpsichord, like the best technical studies, offer an infinite variety of problems of execution, together with real musical merits, of which the latter are too frequently devoid. We cannot sufficiently urge the studious pupil to devote an attentive study to them, for it will especially benefit clearness, precision and lightness ot touch. The numbering adopted is that of the Longo-Ricordi edition.)

	1	2	3	4	5
Nos 20, 103	nd		nd		
Nos 22, 81, 95, 100, 136	nd	nd			
Nos 29, 35	rd	rd		nd	
Nos 32, 102, 115, 127, 149	rd	rd			
No 37	rd	rd	nd		
Nos 43, 104, 139, 175, 200					rd
Nos 50, 155, 188	rd				
Nos 55, 125					nd
Nos 65, 70	nd	nd			nd
Nos 98, 131, 140, 169, 209	nd				
Nos 107, 210, 215, 249			rd		rd
No 109		rd	rd		rd
Nos 157, 241	rd				rd
No 158			rd		
Nos 160, 221	rd		rd		
No 172	rd	rd			rd
No 195	rd	rd	rd		rd
No 232		rd			
No 262		nd			
No 263			rd		

PARADIES 1710-1792

	1	2	3	4	5
Sanata in D. Major (evenness, crossing of hands)	rd	rd			rd

FRENCH SCHOOL

CHAMBONNIÈRES 1600-1670

	1	2	3	4	5
La Verdinguette, gigue (rhythm and grace-notes) (Grovlez-Chester edition)	nd				
Allemande " La Loureuse " n° 11 (grace notes) (Brunold-Senart edition)	nd				
Pavane " L'entretien des Dieux : n° 24 (polyphonic style, grace notes) (Brunold-Senart edition)	nd		nd		
Le Moutier, allemande (sic) (evenness in both hands)	nd	nd			

D'ANGLEBERT 1628-1691

	1	2	3	4	5
Variations sur les Folies d'Espagne (evenness in both hands)	nd				

FR. COUPERIN 1668-1733

(Brahms or Diemer-Durand Edition)

	1	2	3	4	5
1er ordre : La Milordine (evenness)	rd				
L'Enchanteresse (double notes, wrist)	nd		rd		nd
2e ordre : La Florentine (evenness)	nd				
La Diligente (evenness)	rd	nd			
Les Papillons (evenness)	rd				
3e ordre : Les Matelotes provençales (evenness)	nd				
La Lutine (evenness)	rd				
4e ordre : La Pateline (broken double notes)	rd		nd		
Le Réveil-matin (measured tremolo, evenness)	nd				nd
5e ordre : La Tendre Fanchon (polyphonic playing extensions)			rd	nd	
La Bandoline (evenness)	rd				
6e ordre : Les Barricades mystérieuses (legato playing broken double notes)	nd		nd		
Le Moucheron (evenness, lightness)	rd				

	Chapters				
	1	2	3	4	5
9e ordre : Les Charmes (polyphonic playing, double notes, arpeggios)		nd	nd		
Le Bavolet flottant (evenness left hand)	rd				
10e ordre : La Triomphante (1st part) (brio. clearness)	nd	rd			nd
Les Bagatelles (evenness in both hands)	rd				
11e ordre : L'Etincelante ou la Bontemps (evenness)	rd				
La Zénobie (evenness)	rd			nd	
Les Fastes de la grande et ancienne Menestrandise (evenness, tone-colour)	rd	nd			
12e ordre : L'Atalante (evenness in both hands)	rd	nd			
13e ordre : Les Rozeaux (evenness left hand)	rd				
Les Folies françaises ou les Dominos (variat.)	rd	nd			
14e ordre : Le Rossignol en amour (grace notes, trills)	rd				
La Linotte effarouchée (evenness both hands)	rd	nd			
Le Rossignol vainqueur (evenness)	nd				
Le Carillon de Cythère (evenness, grace notes)	rd				
17e ordre : La Superbe ou La Forqueray (evenness)	rd	rd			
Les Petits Moulins à vent (evenness)	rd	nd			
Les Timbres (evenness)	nd	rd			
Les Petites Crémières de Bagnolet (evenness both hands)	rd				
18e ordre : Le Turbulent (evenness)	rd	rd			
Le Tic-toc-choc ou Les Maillotins (cross play)	rd				rd
20e ordre : Les Cherubins (evenness, both hands)	rd	nd			
21e ordre : La Couperin (evenness, polyphonic playing)	rd		d		rd
La Petite Pince-sans-rire (polyphonic playing)			rd		rd
22e ordre : Le Trophée (wrist playing)					rd
Le Point du Jour (evenness)	rd	nd			
L'Anguille (evenness, wrist)	rd				
Les Tours de passe-passe (evenness, wrist)	nd				
23e ordre : Les tricoteuses (evenness finger, staccato)	rd	nd			rd
24e ordre : Les Vieux Seigneurs (grace notes in slow empo)	nd				nd
Les Jeunes Seigneurs (grace notes in rapid tempo)	rd				
Les Brimborions (evenness both hands)	nd	nd			
27e ordre : Saillie (evenness, polyphonic playing)	rd		nd		

DANDRIEU 1684-1740

	1	2	3	4	5
Les Doux Propos (evenness, grace notes)	nd				
Les Cascades (evenness) (Grovlez-Chester edition)	nd				
Les Tourbillons (evenness, lightness of wrist, left hand)	nd				
La Coquète (evenness)	nd				
La Musète (evenness, grace notes) (Brunold-Senart edition)	nd				nd

J. PH. RAMEAU 1683-1764

(Saint-Saëns-Durand edition)

	1	2	3	4	5
La Rappel des Oiseaux (evenness)	rd				
Rigaudon, Musette et Tambourin (in E.) (evenness)	nd				
Les Niais de Sologne (evenness)	nd				
La Joyeuse (evenness both hands)	nd				
Les Tourbillons (evenness both hands)	nd	nd			nd
Les Trois Mains (evenness crossed hands)	rd	rd			rd
Gavotte variée (evenness, polyphonic playing, wrist, extensions)	rd		rd	nd	rd
Les Tricotets (evenness, wrist playing)	nd				nd
La Poule (precision, wrist playing)					nd
L'Egyptienne (evenness)	nd				

DAQUIN 1694-1772

(Senart-Edition)

	1	2	3	4	5
Le Coucou (evenness)	nd				
L'Hirondelle (evenness)	nd				
La Favorite (evenness)	nd				
Les Vents en courroux (evenness, crossed hands)	nd				nd

ENGLISH SCHOOL

W. BYRD 1556-1623

	1	2	3	4	5
The Carman's Whistle (variations, polyphonic style)			nd		
The Bells (evenness, polyphonic playing)		nd	nd		
The Woods so wilde (polyphonic playing)	nd		nd		
John come kiss me now (evenness, polyphonic playing)		nd	rd		

PETER PHILIPS ?-1628

	1	2	3	4	5
Le Rossignol (Orl. de Lassus) (evenness, polyphonic style)	nd	nd	nd		
Galiarda (varied couplets, polyphonic style)	nd		nd		

G. FARNABY 1560-1600?

	1	2	3	4	5
The King's Hunt (evenness)	rd	rd			
Spagnioletta (variations, evenness, repeated notes)	nd	nd			
Daphne (variations, evenness, polyphonic playing)		rd	rd		
Rosalis (variations, evenness)		nd			
Woody-Cock (variations, evenness, polyphonic playing)	rd	rd			

JOHN BULL 1563-1628

	1	2	3	4	5
The Quadran Pavan (polyphonic style, rhythmic difficulties, evenness, both hands)		nd	rd		
Variations of the Quadran Pavan (evenness, both hands)		nd	rd		
Galiard to the Quadran Pavan (double notes, evenness). (It will be interesting to compare this composition with that by Byrd on the same theme)	rd		rd		
The King's Hunt (imitative style, evenness)	rd	rd	nd		

ORLANDO GIBBONS 1583-1625

	1	2	3	4	5
The Woods so wilde (variations, evenness, polyphonic style)	nd	nd	nd		

GERMAN SCHOOL

FROBERGER 1667-1795

	1	2	3	4	5
Toccata in A. Minor (evenness, polyphonic playing)	rd	rd	rd		

J. KUHNAU 1660-1772

	1	2	3	4	5
Partita (or suite) nº 6 A. Major (evenness)	nd	nd			
Sonata seconda in D. Major (Frisches Klavier Früchte)	rd		rd		
Sonates bibliques : nº 1 Fight between David and Goliath	nd	nd	rd		rd
nº 2 Saül cured by David's prowess on the harp (varied technic, descriptive style)	rd		nd		

F. X. MURSCHAUSER 1670-1733

	1	2	3	4	5
Aria pastoralis variata (evenness)	nd	nd			

TELEMAN 1681-1767

	1	2	3	4	5
First Fantasia in D. Major (evenness)	nd				

JEAN-SEBASTIAN BACH 1685-1750

(Steingräber edition)

(Generally speaking, we recommend Steingraber's edition, which is very carefully revised.
We wish to recall the fact that technical considerations alone have been responsible for the choice of the works mentioned in this repertory. Bach's incomparable production, truly the breviary of the pianist musician, bears no selection, from a purely musical standpoint. But here, it is a question of mechanism only.)

	1	2	3	4	5
15 inventions in 2 parts (evenness, running and expressive execution) (analytical editions by Blanche Selva or G. Sporck)	rd	nd			
15 Symphonies or 3 part inventions (evenness polyphonic playing) (analytical editions by Blanche Selva or G. Sporck)	rd	rd	d		
First partita in B ♭. (evenness, lightness of wrist, crossed hands)	rd	rd			rd
Allemande and capriccio (2nd Partita) (evenness, wrist suppleness)	rd	rd			
Courante (5th partita) (evenness, both hands)	d	rd	rd		nd
Italian Concerto (evenness, clearness)					
Chromatic Fantasy and Fugue (complete technique)	d	d	d	rd	rd
Gigue (5th French Suite) (distinct articulation, evenness)	d	rd	rd		
Aria variata alla maniera italiana (6th French Suite) (evenness both hands)	rd	rd	rd		
Prelude (2nd English Suite) (evenness, rhythmic decision)	d	rd			rd
Prelude and fugue in A. Minor (nº 117)					
Prelude, Fugue and Allegro in E ♭. Major					
Fantasy in C. Minor (generous and expressive articulation, crossed hands)	rd	d			rd
Goldberg Variationen (complete technique)	d	d	d	rd	d
Fugue from the Capriccio on the Departure of a Friend (clearness of playing)	d	rd	d		rd
Toccata in F. sharp (evenness, polyphonic playing)	d	d	d		
Toccata in C. Minor (evenness, polyphonic playing)	d	d	d		
Toccata in D. Major (Fantasy and Fugue)	d	d	rd		nd

	1	2	3	4	5
Well-tempered clavichord :					
(Preludes 1st book).					
Nº 1 (evenness, smooth playing)	rd	nd			
Nº 2 (evenness, firm articulation both hands)	d	nd			
Nº 3 (lightness, suppleness of the wrist)	rd				nd
Nº 5 (evenness of the weak fingers)	d	rd			
Nº 6 (evenness right hand)	rd				
Nº 11 (evenness of fingers, lightness of wrist)	d	rd			rd
Nº 14 (evenness of both hands)	rd				nd
Nº 15 (clearness, evenness)	rd	rd			
(Preludes 2nd book.)					
Nº 2 (evenness, neatness of attaek)	rd				nd
Nº 6 (evenness, crossed hands)	rd				rd
Nº 8 (evenness, independence of fingers)	rd				
Nº 10 — — —	rd	rd			
Nº 15 (— — —	rd	nd	rd		
Nº 21 — crossed hands)	rd	rd	rd	rd	nd
Nº 23 (regularity of playing)	rd	nd	nd		nd

(It is superfluous to recommend the study of all the fugues of both books. This constitutes the richest and most varied instruction in polyphonic playing and independence of fingers.)

J. F. HAENDEL 1685-1559

	1	2	3	4	5
1st Suite — Gigue (elasticity of the wrist, evenness of fingers)	rd				rd
3rd Suite — Prelude, Fugue, Air and Variation (evenness, polyphonic playing, grace notes)	rd	nd	rd		
5th Suite — Harmonious Blacksmith (evenness, independence of fingers)	rd	rd	rd		
7th Suite — Passacaglia with variation (clear articulation)	nd	nd			
9th Suite — (clearness, independence of fingers)	nd	rd	rd	rd	
14th Suite — Gavotte with variations (running execution, evenness)	nd				

C. H. GRAUN 1701-1759

	1	2	3	4	5
Gigue in B. *b* Minor (evenness, crossed hands)	rd				rd

2. - Transition from the harpsichord to the pianoforte

W. FRIED. BACH 1710-1784

	1	2	3	4	5
Capriccio in D. Minor (wrist evenness, polyphonic playing)	nd		rd		nd
Fugue in C. Minor	rd		rd		
Polonaise in G. *b*. (legato playing)	nd		nd		
Polonaise in E. Minor (polyphonic playing, extensions) (Philipp-Durand edition)			rd	rd	

PH. EMMANUEL BACH 1714-1788

	1	2	3	4	5
Allegro in A. Major (wrist evenness)		rd			rd
Wurtenberg sonata in A *b*. op. 2 (evenness, expressive playing)	rd		rd		
Wurtenberg sonata in B. minor (evenness, expressive playing)	rd		rd		

T. P. KIRNBERGER 1721-1783

	1	2	3	4	5
Fugue in 2 voices in D. major (evenness)	rd	rd			
Fugue in 3 voices in D. minor (extensions, evenness polyphonic playing)	rd		rd	rd	
Courante in A. *b*. major (evenness, both hands)	rd	rd			
Allegro für die Singuhr (carrillon) (evenness, stretches)	nd			nd	

JOH. CHRISTIAN BACH 1735-1782

	1	2	3	4	5
Prelude ang fugue in C. minor			rd		
Finale sonata in B. *b*. major (evenness)	rd	rd			

JOSEPH HAYDN 1732-1809

The study of all the Haydn Sonatas is recommended with a view to a light, expressive, and spirited execution. Let us however mention, as being most efficacious for exercising the fingers, the following numbers : (Peter's edition)

	1	2	3	4	5
Sonata nº 1 (in its entirety ; expressive and running execution)	rd	rd			nd

Chapters	1	2	3	4	5
Sonata nº 2 Adagio (expressive, grace notes)	nd	nd			
Sonata nº 7 Allegro (evenness, rhythmic precision)	rd	nd			rd
Sonata nº 8 (in its entirely, volubility, evenness)	rd	rd			nd
Sonata nº 9 Finale (lightness of the wrist)	nd				rd
Sonata nº 12 Presto (lightness, suppleness of wrist)	nd				rd
Sonata nº 19 (in its entirety, precision, lightness, evenness)	rd	rd			rd
Sonata nº 23 Finale (lightness of fingers and wrist)	nd	nd			rd
Andante with variations in F. minor (evenness, grace notes, crossed hands)	rd	rd			nd
Arietta con variazioni (finger technique)	rd	rd			nd
Fantasia in C. major (evenness, wrist)	rd	rd	nd		rd

W. A. MOZART 1756-1791

Sonatas (numbered according to the Peters edition) :

	1	2	3	4	5
Nº 1 in A (evenness, variety of playing, legato and staccato)	rd	rd			nd
Nº 2 in C (refined and running execution)	nd	rd			nd
Nº 3 in D (brilliant playing, clearness, rhythmic precision)	rd	rd			nd
Nº 6 in F (finale) (volubility, clearness)	rd	rd			nd
Nº 7 in A minor (allegro maestoso) (firmness, precision)	rd	rd	rd		rd
Nº 10 in D major (brio, clearness, evenness, crossed hands)	rd	rd			rd
Nº 12 in A major (expressive virtuosity) (finale « Alla Turca ») (brio, rhythm)	rd	rd			rd
Nº 13 in D major (lightness, clearness, evenness)	rd	rd			
Nº 17 in B *b*. (allegro) (evenness, elegant playing)	nd	nd			
(For the analytical study of these sonatas, we recommend George Sporck's edition)					
Rondo in A. minor (evenness expressive style)	rd	rd	d	rd	
Rondo F. major (grace notes, evenness)	d	rd	rd		rd
Fantasy in C. minor followed by a sonata (varied technique dramatic style)	rd	d			rd
Fantasy in C. major with fugue	d	d	d	rd	d
Gigue in G. major (wrist suppleness, clearness, lightness)			rd	rd	d

M. CLEMENTI 1752-1832

	1	2	3	4	5
Gradus and Parnassum (selections to be made by the teacher ; complete finger technique)					
Sonata op. 5 (broken octaves, evenness, crossing hands)	rd	rd		rd	d
Sonata op. 47. Finale (evenness, broken thirds)	d	rd	d		
(The best edition of Clementi's sonatas is that of Gastoué-Senart)					
6th Canon in two parts (suppleness of wrist, substitution of fingers) (Bl. Selva's edition)	d				d

J. L. DUSSEK 1761-1812

	1	2	3	4	5
Sonata « The return to Paris » (varied technique)	d	d	d		rd

3. - The Pianoforte

When the pianoforte became universally adopted, keyboard technique underwent a radical transformation. The variety of sentiments expressed by a broader and wealthier instrumental style demanded not only a diversity of means for their translation, but also the use of multiple combinations of writing in a single piece. It therefore becomes difficult from Beethoven onwards, to assign a definite place to the works whose classification we have undertaken, in a programme of study based on the specialization of their difficulties. We shall therefore, at times, only retain certain salient passages in these works, in order to render their entry into one or other of the chapters of this volume, legitimate. It does not follow from this, that other fragments of the same work are not worthy of similar attention, nor that they cannot be the objects of work of the same nature. We leave to the perspicacity of the teacher, the completion of such parts of our work as are inevitably rudimentary, limited as we are by considerations of a purely technical order.

L. VAN BEETHOVEN 1770-1827

	1	2	3	4	5
Sonata op. 2, nº 1. Finale.	rd	rd	nd	rd	rd
— op. 2, nº 2. Allegro vivace and Rondo	rd	d	rd	rd	d
— op. 2, nº 3. (in its entirety)	nd	rd		rd	d

	Chapters 1	2	3	4	5
Sonata op. 7 Rondo	rd	nd		rd	rd
— op. 10 nº 1. Finale	rd	rd	nd	nd	rd
— op. 10 nº 2. Allegro and presso	rd	rd	rd	rd	d
— op. 10 nº 3. Presto largo	rd	rd	rd	rd	rd
— op. 13 known as the Pathetic (in its entirety).	rd	nd	d	rd	rd
— op. 14 nº 1. Rondo.	rd	rd			
— op. 14 nº 2. Scherzo	rd	nd			d
— op. 22 Allegro con brio.	d	d	rd	rd	nd
— op. 26 in its entirety (especially the finale).	d	d	d	rd	rd
— op. 27 nº 1, Quasi una fantasia	rd	d	rd	rd	d
— op. 27 nº 2		d	d	d	rd
— op. 28, in its entirety.		rd	d	rd	d
— op. 31 nº 1, Allegro vivace	d	rd			rd
— op. 31 nº 2 in its entirety	d	d			d
— op. 31 nº 3, Scherzo and presto con fuoco		rd			d
— op. 53, in its entirety.	d	d		d	d
— op. 54, —		d	d		d
— op. 57, known As the appassionata	d	vd	d	d	vd
— op. 78		d			d
— op. 81 « Les Adieux, l'Absence, le Retour »	d	vd	d	d	d
— op. 101		vd	vd	vd	d
— op. 106 (complete technique).	vd	vd	vd	vd	vd
— op. 109	d	d	d	v	d
— op. 110	vd	vd	d	vd	d
— p. 111	vd	vd	vd	vd	vd
(For the study of these sonatas we recommend A. Casella's edition).					
Rondo op. 51, nº 2	d	d			
Andante F. major	rd		d		d
15 Varitions with fugue op. 35	d	d	vd		d
33 Variations on a theme by Diabelli (complete transcendent technique).	vd	vd	vd	vd	vd
32 Variations in G. minor	d	vd	d	d	d

J. N. HUMMEL 1778-1837

	1	2	3	4	5
Sonata in E *b*. op. 13.	d	d	rd		
Sonata in F. sharp minor op. 81	d	d	d	rd	d

CH. M. VON WEBER 1786-1826

	1	2	3	4	5
Sonata op. 24 in C. major.					
Allegro (bravura, brio, wrist technique)		d	d	vd	vd
Scherzo (lightness, thirds, wrist suppleness extensions).			d	vd	d
Rondo, perpetuum mobile (evenness, volubility).	d	d	d		d
Sonata op. 39 in A *b*. major (complete technique)	d	d	d	vd	d
Sonata op. 49 in D. minor (complete technique especially in the Finale	d	vd	vd	d	vd
Momento capriccioso op. 12 (wrist double notes).		d	vd		vd
Polonaise op. 21 (brilliancy, rhythmic precision).	d	rd	d	d	d
Rondo brillant op. 62 (elegant virtuosity, evenness, wrist suppleness)	d	d			d
Invitation to waltz (brio, poetry, vitality of execution).	d	d		d	d

F. SCHUBERT 1797-1828

	1	2	3	4	5
Sonata op. 42, Andante	d	vd	d	d	d
— — Rondo (evenness, wrist suppleness)	d	d			d
Sonata op. 53, Allegro (evenness of both hands).	d	d		rd	rd
— op. 122, Allegro moderato (Finale) (extensions polyphonic playing).	d		d	vd	
— op. 143, Allegro vivace (evenness of both hands, volubility)	vd	d			d
Sonata in A major (without nº) Schezzo (wrist playing crossed hands)			rd		vd
Fantasy op. 15 Der Wanderer » (complete technique)	d	vd	vd	d	vd
Menuetto of op. 18 (wrist, 2 part playing).			d	d	d
Impromptus op. 90 :					
Nº 2 in E. *b*. (evenness, extensions).	d	d		d	
Nº 4 in A. *b* (substitution of fingers, lightness, chords).	d	d		d	
Impromptus op. 142 :					
Nº 3 variations	d	vd		d	
Nº 4 in F. minor (wrist, velocity).		d	d		d

C. CZERNY 1791-1857

	1	2	3	4	5
Fugues.	d	d	vd	vd	
Study Sonata.	d	d	vd	d	d
Toccata in C. op. 92 (double notes).	d		vd		

F. MENDELSSOHN 1809-1847

	1	2	3	4	5
Songs without words :					
Op. 19, nº 3 « The Hunt » (brilliant rhythm, wrist ,evenness).		d	rd		d
Op' 30, nº 2 (independence of fingers in double notes playing			d		d
Op. 30, nº 4 (repetitions, wrist suppleness)		rd		rd	d
Op. 30, nº 5 (evenness, left hand)		d	rd		
Op. 38, nº 3 (extensions, accompaniment shared by both hands)		rd		d	rd
Op. 38 nº 6 Duetto (expressive independence of fingers).		rd		d	
Op. 53, nº 3 (evenness in extensions)		rd		rd	
— nº 4 (extensions, expressive playing).				d	
— nº 6 (alternation, wrist chords)			rd	rd	d
Op. 62 nº 1 (legato and expressive playing, evenness of accompaniment).	rd			rd	rd
Op. 62, nº 6 « Spring song » (evenness, suppleness).		rd		rd	rd
Op. 67, nº 2 (independence of articulation)			rd	d	rd
— n 4 « La Fileuse » (evenness, lightness)	d	d			rd
Op. 85, nº 6 (independence of fingers)			d	d	rd
Op. 102, nº 3 (wrist suppleness, precision in attack).	rd		rd		d
Capriccio in F. sharp minor op. 5 (evenness, lightness, velocity)	d	d	d		rd
Charakterstûcke op. 7 :					
Nº 1 (polyphonic style)			rd	d	
Nº 2 (evenness of both hands)	d	d			
Nº 3 (Fugato style, precision, independence of fingers)	d	d	d	d	
Nº 4 (evenness, running execution)	d	d		rd	
Nº 7 (lightness of wrist, alternation)	d		rd		vd
Rondo capriccioso (lightness, vivacity)	d	d			d
Capriccio op. 16, nº 2, Scherzo (lightness of wrist, evenness).	d	d			d
Presto of the fantasy op. 28 (evenness, velocity).	d	d			rd
Preludes and fugues op. 35 :					
Nº 1. Prelude (alternation, arpeggios)		d		rd	d
— Fugue (ornemental polyphonic style).		d	d	rd	d
Nº 3 Prelude (light staccato).		d			d
Nº 6 Prelude (chord technique)				d	rd
Variations sérieuses op. 34 (varied technique).	d	d	rd	d	d
3 Preludes and 3 Studies op. 104 (various difficulties).	d	d	d	d	d
Scherzo of the sonata op. 106 (light staccatto)	d		d		d
Perpetuum mobile op. 119 (evenness velocity)	d	d			

FR. CHOPIN 1810-1849

Not a single work of Chopin's should be omitted for the education of a pianist, for none has known better nor more musically than he, how to make the most of the instrument's resources. The restraint which we regretfully impose upon ourselves, forces us only to take into account those pieces most profitable to the technical progress of the student.

	1	2	3	4	5
Studies op. 10 :					
Nº 1 (strength of the fingers, extensions).		vd		vd	d
Nº 2 (independence and evenness of the weak fingers).		vd	vd	d	d
Nº 3 (polyphonic playing extensions).			d	vd	d
Nº 4 (evenness of fingers, velocity, brio)	d	d	vd	d	d
Nº 5 (on the black keys, clearness and volubility).	vd	vd	d	d	d
Nº 6 (expressive polyphonic playing).			d	d	d
Nº 7 (mobility and agility of the fingers in double notes).	d		vd	d	d
Nº 8 (lightness and evenness in thumb transmission).	d	vd		d	d
Nº 9 (left hand extensions, right hand expressive declamation).				d	d
Nº 10 (wrist and hand suppleness, extensions)			d	vd	vd
Nº 11 (chords, arpeggios, extensions, wrist suppleness)			d	vd	vd
Nº 12 (left hand force and volubility, right hand, chord technique)	vd	vd		d	d
Studies op. 25 :					
Nº 1 (evenness, delicacy, extensions)	d	vd		d	d
Nº 2 (evenness, light finger action right hand)	vd	vd			
Nº 3 (neatness and independence of fingers, wrist suppleness).	d		d	d	vd
Nº 4 (chord technique, wrist suppleness).			d	d	vd
Nº 5 (thumb transmission, extensions, wrist)		d	d	d	vd
Nº 6 (thirds, independence, evenness of fingers).	d	vd	vd	d	d
Nº 7 (legato playing, expressive polyphonic technique)		d	d	d	
Nº 8 (sixths, evenness, extensions).	vd		vd	vd	d
Nº 9 (wrist octaves, lightness, precision).			vd	d	vd
Nº 10 (legato octaves, wrist resistance)			vd	vd	vd
Nº 11 (force and volubility, extension between fingers)	vd	vd		vd	d
Nº 12 (displacement of the hand on the key-board, stretches, finger resistance).		vd		d	vd
Ballads :					
Nº 1 op. 23 in G. minor (complete technique)	d	d	d	vd	vd
Nº 2 op. 38 in F. major (double notes, wrist).			vd	vd	vd
Nº 3 op. 47 in A. *b*. (complete technique)	d	d	d	vd	vd
Nº 4 op. 52 in F. minor (polyphonic playing, double notes)	d	d	vd	vd	vd
Impromptus :					
Op. 29 (evenness, both hands)	d	d		d	
Op. 36 (wrist evenness, wrist left hand).	d	d		rd	d

	Chapters 1	2	3	4	5
Op. 51 (equality)	d	d	vd	d	
Impromptu Fantasy in C. sharp minor (evenness, velocity)	d	vd			
Scherzos :					
Op. 28 (extensions, evenness)	d	d		vd	d
Op. 31 (complete technique)	d	d	d	d	vd
Op. 39 (wrist, broken formulae)	d	d		d	vd
Op. 54 (lightness of execution, wrist)	d	d	rd	d	d
Fantasy op. 49 (complete technique)	d	vd	d	d	vd
Preludes op. 28 :					
Nº 1 (extensions, articulation independence)		d	d	d	rd
Nº 2 (extensions left hand)				d	
Nº 3 (evenness, lightness left hand)	d	vd			
Nº 5 (stretches, evenness playing)	vd	d		vd	
Nº 8 (independence and resistance of fingers)	vd	vd		d	d
Nº 12 (firmness of fingers, wrist suppleness)	d	d	d	d	vd
Nº 14 (evenness of both hands)	d	d			
Nº 16 (brilliancy, velocity, right hand resistance left hand wrist)	vd	vd			vd
Nº 17 (chord technique, extensions)			d	d	d
Nº 18 (impetuous execution, force and agility of both hands)	vd	vd			d
Nº 19 (lightness, continuous extensions for both hands)		vd		vd	d
Nº 23 (thumb transmission, right hand, light and fluid execution)	vd	vd		d	d
Waltz :					
Op. 64, nº 1 (evenness, velocity, lightness)	d	d			
Polonaises :					
Op. 40, nº 1 (chord technique, firmness, brilliant rhyhthm)			d	d	d
Op. 44, — — —		d		d	d
Op. 53 (chord and wrist technique, octaves left hand)	d	d	d	vd	vd
Polonaise fantasy (polyphonic playing, chord technique)			vd	d	vd
Nocturnes :					
Op. 25, nº 2 (grace-notes, extensions right hand)	vd	d		d	vd
Op. 37, nº 2 (expressive double notes)	d		vd		
Op. 48, nº 1 (octave and chord technique)				vd	vd
Op. 55, nº 2 (polyphonic playing, stretching left hand)	d		d	d	
Sonatas :					
Op. 35, 1st movement (chord and extension technique)		d	vd	vd	vd
— Scherzo (wrist suppleness double notes and chords)		d	vd	d	vd
— Finale (evenness, lightness, velocity of both hands)	vd	vd			d
Op. 58, 1st movement (extension technique)		d	d	vd	d
— Scherzo (velocity, lightness)	vd	vd			
— Finale (complete technique)	vd	d	d	vd	vd
Berceuse (evenness, fluidity, suppleness)	vd	d	d	d	d
Barcarolle (polyphonic playing, double notes and chords)	d	vd	vd	d	d
Tarentella (brilliancy, vivacity, clearness)	d	d	rd	d	
Concert allegro (complete technique)	vd	d	vd	vd	d
Studies for the Moscheles method :					
Nº 2 (chord technique)			d	d	d
Nº 3 (polyphonic playing, articulation, precision)	d		vd	d	d

(Mikuli's edition is supposed to conform the most closely with the original text. The Peters and Breitkopf editions are also to be recommended. For the studies, Preludes and Ballads we take the liberty of mentioning the Student's edition, brought out under our name by Senart.)

R. SCHUMANN 1810-1856

(Breitkopf edition revised by Clara Schumann)

(The incomparable musical interest attached to the study of all Schumann's pianistic works is not always accompanied, for the executant, by its technical equivalent. Save for some rare exceptions, his writings belong to the polyphonic style, and pure virtuosity has few opportunities of manifesting itselt.

This explains our limited choice, determined by the specialized tendencies of this repertory.)

	Chapters 1	2	3	4	5
Variations on the name of « Abbegg » op. 1 (independence of fingers, 2 part playing)	d	vd	d	d	
Studies after Paganini op. 3 :					
Nº 1 (evenness, clearness, finger strength)	d	vd			
Nº 2 (double notes, wrist)	d		d	rd	d
Nº 4 (double notes, extensions, wrist play)				d	vd
Nº 6 (finger independence, firm playing)	d	vd	d	d	
Intermezzo op. 4, nº 6 (independence of fingers)	d	d		d	d
Impromptus (in variations) op. 5 1st version (technique of double notes and chords)	d		vd	vd	vd
Davids Bündler Tänze op. 6 :					
Nº 6 (finger independence of the left hand)	vd		d	rd	vd
Nº 9 (firmness of the weak fingers, wrist suppleness)	d		d	d	vd
Nº 12 (wrist suppleness)	d		d		d
Toccata op. 7 (study of double notes)	d		vd	vd	vd
Allegro op. 8 (polyphonic style, technique of stretches)	d	d	d	vd	d
Carnival op. 9 (varied technique, especially chords and wrist)	d	d	d	d	vd
Six concert studies op. 10 (after Paganini especially chords wrist, independence of fingers)	d	vd	d	d	vd
Phantasiestücke op. 12 « Traümen Wirren » (Hallucinations) (equality of fingers, wrist suppleness)	d			d	vd
Symphony studies op. 13 (chord and wrist technique)			vd	d	vd
Kreisleriana op. 16 :					
Nº 1 (strength of fingers, extensions, suppleness of wrist)	vd			vd	d
Nº 3 (neat articulation, suppleness of wrist)	d			d	vd
Nº 7 (strength of fingers in rapid emission)	vd	d		d	d
Nº 8 (finger independence, wrist suppleness)	d		d		vd
Fantasy op. 17 2nd part (chord technique, wrist play)			d	d	vd
Humoresque op. 20 (varied technique)	vd	d	d	d	vd
Novelette op. 21 :					
Nº 2 (strength of fingers, suppleness of wrist, clear articulation)	vd		d	d	vd
Nº 7 (octaves wrist play)			d	d	d
Nº 8 (varied technique)	d		d		vd
Sonata op. 22 :					
1st movement (extensions, strength of fingers, volubility)	vd	d		d	d
Rondo (wrist suppleness, evenness of fingers)	d			d	vd
Nachtstücke op. 23 nº 4 (chords, arpeggios, extensions)				d	rd
Viennese Carnival op. 26 :					
Allegro (strength of fingers, elasticity of wrist)	d			d	d
Intermezzo (crossed hands, evenness, buoyancy)	d			d	d
Finale (brilliancy, neat articulation, wrist)	d	d	rd		d
Romance op. 28 nº 1 (change of hands, evenness firmness)	d			d	d
Romance of the op. 32 (evenness and independence of wrist movements)			d	d	vd
Fuguettes op. 126 nºs 4 and 6 (articulated polyphony)	d	vd	d		
Gesande der Frühe (Morning songs) op. 133 nº 4 (distribution of melody in both hands, articulation)	d	d		d	d

FR. LISZT 1811-1886

One might here reverse the preceding observation, on the pianistic style of Schumann. Liszt's inventive virtuosity is so abundantly exercised in all his compositions, that selection becomes difficult. We shall only mention the most significant of his works, counting on the professors for the amendment, according to their personal preferences of the voluntary omissions we are obliged to make.

	Chapters 1	2	3	4	5
Transcendental Studies :					
Nº 1 Preludio (bravura, strength of fingers, extensions)		vd	d	vd	d
Nº 2 in A. minor (wrist suppleness, alternate playing)	d	vd	d	vd	vd
Nº 3 Landscape (expressive technique of double notes and chords)			d	d	d
Nº 4 Mazeppa (impetuosity, wrist, chord and double note technique)		d	vd	vd	vd
Nº 5 Will-of-the-wisp (varied double notes, wrist suppleness)	vd	vd	vd	vd	d
Nº 6 Vision (crossed hands, arpeggios, picked out chords, extensions)		vd		vd	vd
Nº 7 Eroica (octaves, arpeggios, extensions)		vd		vd	vd
Nº 8 Wilde Jagd (wild Hunt) (chords, wrist, extensions)			d	vd	vd
Nº 9 Ricordanza (grace notes, arpeggios)	vd	vd		d	d
Nº 10 in F. minor (wrist supplenness, octaves, extensions)	d	vd		vd	vd
Nº 11 Evening harmonies (chord technique and arpeggios)			d	vd	vd
Nº 12 The snow-plough (tremolo, extension, wrist)	vd	vd		vd	vd
Studies after Paganini :					
Nº 1 (scales, arpeggios, tremolos, extensions)		vd		vd	vd
Nº 2 (alternation, crossed hands, octaves, wrist)	vd	vd	vd		vd
Nº 3 La Campanella (wrist, leaps, evenness, volubility)	vd	vd	d	vd	vd
Nº 4 (crossed hands, lightness and suppleness of wrist)	vd	vd	vd		vd
Nº 5 (double notes, alternating glissandi, quick displacement of hand)	vd		vd	d	vd
Nº 6 Variations (varied technique, especially wrist)	vd	vd	vd	vd	vd
Concert studies (3) :					
Nº 2 La Leggierezza (evenness, smooth and rapid playing, double notes)	vd	vd	vd	d	d
Nº 3 Il Sospiro (crossed hands, arpeggios, evenness)	d	vd	d	d	d
Concert studies (2) :					
1 Waldesrauschen (broken chords, evenness)	d	d		vd	d
2 Gnomen reigen (lightness, precision, wrist suppleness)	vd	vd	d		vd
Ab Irato (study for the achievement of high finish)		vd	vd	vd	vd
Hungarian Rhapsodies :					
Nº 2 (varied technique, bravura, brilliancy)	d	d	vd	d	vd
Nº 4 (evenness, volubility, staccato octaves)	vd	d	d	d	vd
Nº 6 (chord technique, wrist octaves)		vd		d	vd
Nº 8 (varied technique, volubility, bravura)	vd	vd		d	vd
Nº 9 (complete technique)	vd	vd	vd	vd	vd
Nº 10 (wrist technique, glissando)		d	vd	vd	vd

	Chapters				
	1	2	3	4	5
Nº 11 (varied technique, fingers and wrist)	vd	d	d	d	vd
Nº 12 (complete technique)	vd	d	vd	d	vd
Nº 13 (varied technique, repeated notes and wrist)	vd	d	vd	d	vd
Nº 14 (complete technique)	vd	d	d	d	vd
Nº 15 Rakoczy-Marsch (bravura, brilliancy, chord technique)	vd	vd		d	vd
Spanish Rhapsody (brio, clearness, chords)	d		vd	vd	vd
Years of Pilgrimage :					
Switzerland. Beside a spring (equality, wrist suppleness)	vd	vd	vd	d	d
O storm (octave technique)			d	d	vd
Valley of Obermann (wrist resistance, extensions)			d	vd	vd
Italy. After a reading of Dante (chord and octave technique)			d	vd	vd
The playing of the waters at the Villa d'Este (equality, tremolos)	vd		d	d	vd
Tarantella (Venezia e Napoli) (wrist technique, fioritures, double notes)	vd	d	d		vd
Sonata in B. minor (complete technique)	vd	vd	d	vd	vd
Legends :					
Nº 1, St-Francis of Assisi : Sermon to the Birds (equality, lightness, trills and tremolos)	vd		d		d
Nº 2, St-Francis of Paul walking on the waters (left hand chord technique)	d	vd	d		vd
2nd Polonaise (bravura, octaves evenness, double notes)	vd	vd	vd	d	d
Mephisto-Walzer (wrist technique)		d	d		vd
Religious and Poetical harmonies :					
Blessing of God in solitude (double notes extensions)			vd	d	
Throughts of the dead (chord technique, wrist resistance)				d	vd
Lullaby (grace notes, evenness, lightness, double notes)	vd	vd	vd		
Fantasy and fugue on the name B.A.C.H. (polyphonic technique, octave playing)		d	vd	d	vd
Concert-solo (varied technique)	d	vd	d		vd
Scherzo and March (chords and wrist)	vd	vd	d	d	vd
Variations on Weinen, Klagen, Sorgen (polyphonic style)			d	vd	vd
(We do not speak of the numberless transcriptions and paraphrases, in which, however, useful matter for technical study can be found. We will nevertheless make an exception in favour of the fantasy on Don Juan, which combines powerful and daring musical merits with its qualities of transcendant virtuosity.)					

J. BRAHMS 1833-1897

	1	2	3	4	5
Variations and Fugue on a theme by Haendel (complete technique with predominance of chord playing and double notes)	d	vd	vd	d	d
Variations on a theme by Paganini (2 books) (complete technique, predominance of double notes and wrist playing)	vd	vd	vd	vd	vd
Sonata op. 5 (technique of chords, extensions, and the wrist)	d	vd	d	vd	vd
Variations on a theme by Schumann (polyphonic technique, chords and double notes)		d	d	d	d
Variations on an original theme op. 21, nº 1 (technique of chords and extensions)		vd	d	vd	d
Capriccio op. 76, nº 2 (independence of fingers, precision in staccato)	d		d	d	d
Rhapsody op. 79, nº 2 (breadth of play, crossed hands)			d	d	d
Intermezzo op. 117 nº 2 (expressive evenness)	d	d		d	d
Ballad op. 118, nº 3 (chord technique, wrist play)			d	d	d
Intermezzo op. 118, nº 6 (evenness left hand, octaves)	d	vd			d
Intermezzo op. 119, nº 3 (polyphonic playing suppleness of wrist, clear articulation)			d	d	vd
Studies from Chopin (thirds and sixths legato)			vd	d	
Rondo from Weber (perpetuum mobile for the left hand)	vd	vd			d
Presto from Bach 2 versions (evenness of both hands, strength and independence of fingers)	vd	vd			
Chaconne from Bach (for the left hand alone)	vd	d	d	vd	d

C. FRANCK 1822-1890

	1	2	3	4	5
Prelude, Choral and Fugue (polyphonic playing, evenness, crossing hands)	d	d	d	vd	d
Prelude, Aria and Finale (polyphonic technique, wrist)		d		vd	d

Without entering into the details of the contemporary masters' works, and leaving aside the productions of living composers, we must nevertheless draw the teacher's attention to the compositions of Ch. V. Alkan, of Balakirew, of Grieg, of Fauré, of Saint-Saëns, of Debussy, of Albeniz, of Granados, etc..., which all deserve to figure in the repertories of pianists.

Another word of advice after so many for which we make our apologies. Experience has taught us that the best way of stimulating the progress of pupils is always to allow place, in their plan of work, for the study of a piece whose difficulty is definitely beyond their attainments. It will be well not to insist on an irreproachable execution of this systematically "too difficult" work whose choice must often be renewed. On the other hand an execution, perfect in every way, must be exacted in the works not exceeding the pupils capacity.